What's New
Microsoft Office Project 2007

Dale A. Howard
Gary L. Chefetz

What's New
Microsoft Office Project 2007

Publisher: Soho Corp dba MSProjectExperts
Authors: Dale A. Howard and Gary L. Chefetz
Cover Design: Tony Valenzuela
Copy Editor: Rodney L. Walker
Cover Photo: Peter Hurley

ISBN 978-1-934240-04-5

Library of Congress Control Number: 2007930474

Published and distributed by Soho Corp. dba MSProjectExperts, 90 John Street, Suite 404, New York, NY 10038. (646) 736-1688 http://www.msprojectexperts.com

EPM Learning™

EPM Learning™ is a complete series of role-based training/reference manuals for Microsoft's Enterprise Project Management software including Microsoft Office Project and Microsoft Office Project Server. Use our books for self-study or for classroom learning delivered by professional trainers and corporate training programs. To learn more about the EPM Learning™ courseware series for Administrators, Implementers, Project Managers, Resource Managers, Executives, Team Members, and Developers, or to obtain instructor companion products and materials, contact MSProjectExperts by phone (646) 736-1688 or by email info@msprojectexperts.com.

Contents

Contents

iv

Introduction

Thank you for choosing *What's New Microsoft Office Project 2007.* We designed this book as a quick learning guide to get you up to speed with the new features in Microsoft Office Project 2007. The content of this book derives from the *Ultimate Learning Guide to Microsoft Office Project 2007*, (ISBN: 978-1-934240-00-7) published 1/15/2007. Consider obtaining *The Ultimate Learning Guide* for a complete learning experience and reference manual, which includes the new features in Project 2007 presented in context with Project Management Institute (PMI) best practices and project management cycle.

Microsoft Office Project 2007 functionality remains mostly unchanged from its 2000-series predecessors; however, Microsoft added a few select features that greatly enhance Project's usability. Perhaps the most potent new feature is the long awaited multi-level undo capability. You can now set your application to support up to 100 levels of undo, and Microsoft added support for undoing macros. For project managers who spend much of their time using Microsoft Project, this feature alone, makes an upgrade worthwhile.

The 2007 edition introduces two additional planning support features to make your life easier. These include Task Change Highlighting and the new Task Drivers pane. Task Change Highlighting instantly highlights all affected tasks in your schedule to indicate the impact of the changes as you make them. The new Task Drivers pane provides you with instant feedback when you need to determine the factors driving a task start date. Finally, the new Visual Reports feature delivers the type of robust reporting capabilities that Project Managers have been yearning for since Project's introduction.

Numerous smaller and more subtle enhancements round out the changes in Project 2007 and we cover these changes as well, after exploring the meat and potatoes. Enjoy!

Download the Sample Files

Before working on any of the Hands-On Exercises in this book, you must download and unzip the sample files required for each exercise. You can download these sample files from the following URL:

http://www.msprojectexperts.com/whatsnew

Module 01

What's New Project Planning

Learning Objectives

After completing this module, you will be able to:

- Use the new Microsoft Office Project 2007 templates to define a project

- Be familiar with the six-step method for defining a new project in Microsoft Office Project 2007

- Create and edit base calendars

- Use the new Microsoft Office Project 2007 option for setting the number of Undo levels

Using Microsoft Office Project 2007 Templates

To define a new project, you may need to begin with a new template. You should use this 4-step method to create a new template, in Microsoft Office Project 2007:

1. Click Project ➢ Project. The software opens a sidepane on the left-hand side of the screen, called the *New Project* sidepane.

2. Click on the *On computer* link, which opens up the Templates dialog.

3. Click the *Project Templates* tab, which displays a list of all the pre-installed (default) templates that ship with the software. Microsoft Office Project 2007 ships with 41 templates, many of which are new to the 2007 version. This list also contains project templates that you saved for future use.

4. Select a template most appropriate for your new project and click the *OK* button.

 MSProjectExperts recommends that you establish a naming convention for templates that enables you to distinguish your organization's customized templates from the default templates that ship with Microsoft Office Project 2007. For example, if you begin the name of all customized templates with an underscore character, the initial underscore pushes all customized templates to the top of the display list in the Templates dialog.

Hands On Exercise

Exercise 1-1

Create a new project from a project template.

1. Launch Project 2007 (If you are using Project Professional, select the *Computer* profile and click the *OK* button).
2. Click File ➤ New, the systems opens the *New Project* sidepane.
3. In the Templates section, click the *On computer* link.
4. In the Templates dialog, select the *Project Templates* tab.
5. Select any of the built-in project templates displayed in the window and double-click on it or click the *Open* button.
6. Review your new schedule.
7. Close your new schedule without saving it.

Defining a New Project

After you determine your project requirements, you are ready to define the project in Microsoft Office Project 2007 using the MSProjectExperts recommended six-step method. You should use this six-step method when you begin a new project from a blank slate or create a new project from a project template. Steps 1-3 are the same steps you used in prior versions of the software. The process for Step 4 is completely new in Microsoft Office Project 2007, and there are new features in Step 5.

The six-step method includes the following mandatory and optional steps:

1. Set the project Start date.

2. Enter the project Properties.

3. Display the Project Summary Task (Row 0).

4. Set the project working schedule.

5. Set project Options unique to this project (optional).

6. Save the project according to your company's naming standards.

After completing the six-step definition process, you are ready to begin the task planning process.

Creating and Editing Base Calendars

The process in Step 4 in the six-step method, setting the Project Working Schedule, is completely new in Microsoft Office Project 2007. Using this process, you must modify the Standard calendar in your project to reflect your company's working schedule. Project 2007 cannot produce a valid schedule until you account for working times and company holidays in the calendar. To modify the Standard calendar in a project, complete the following steps:

1. Click Tools ➢ Change Working Time.

The software opens the Change Working Time dialog, as shown in Figure 1-1.

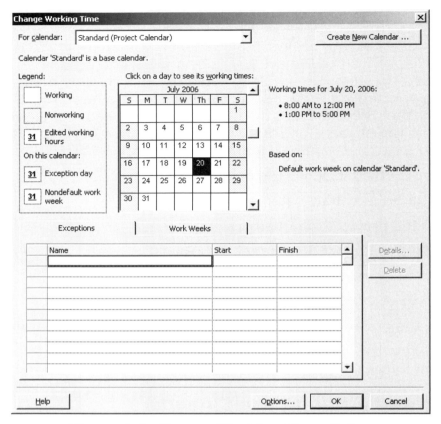

Figure 1-1: Change Working Time dialog

2. In the calendar data grid, select the date of the next company holiday, such as Labor Day, for example.

To set consecutive nonworking days, drag your mouse pointer to select a block of days. To select noncontiguous dates, select the first date, press and hold the *Ctrl* key to select additional dates.

3. On the new *Exceptions* tab in the bottom half of the page, enter a name for the holiday, such as Labor Day, and then press the Tab key.

Microsoft Office Project 2007 sets the date as a company holiday, as shown in Figure 1-2.

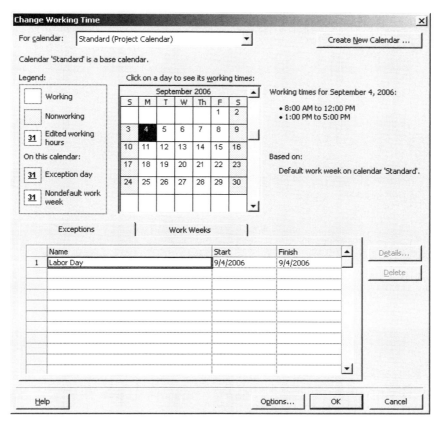

**Figure 1-2: Labor Day set as
company holiday**

4. Click the *Details* button.

The software displays the Details dialog for the selected holiday, as shown in
Figure 1-3.

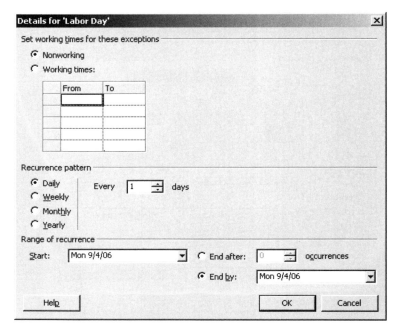

**Figure 1-3: Details dialog before
setting Labor Day recurrence**

5. In the Recurrence Pattern section, select the *Yearly* option and then select your pattern of recurrence.

6. In the *Range of Recurrence* section, select the *End after* option and then select the number of years for which you wish the software to set the holiday (such as 10 years, for example).

Figure 1-4 shows that I set the *Recurrence pattern* values to *Yearly* on the *First Monday* of *September* (the official date of Labor Day every year) and set the *Range of recurrence* values to *End after* 10 *occurrences*.

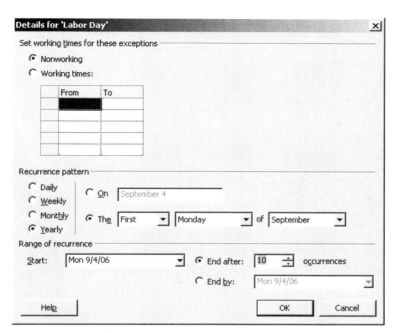

**Figure 1-4: Details dialog after
setting Labor Day recurrence**

7. Click the *OK* button.

8. Repeat steps #1-7 for each company holiday.

9. Click the *OK* button.

After you set your holidays on the Standard calendar, Microsoft Office Project 2007 schedules no task work on a date specified as a company holiday. Figure 1-5 shows the Change Working Time dialog after I set Labor Day as a nonworking day for the next 10 years.

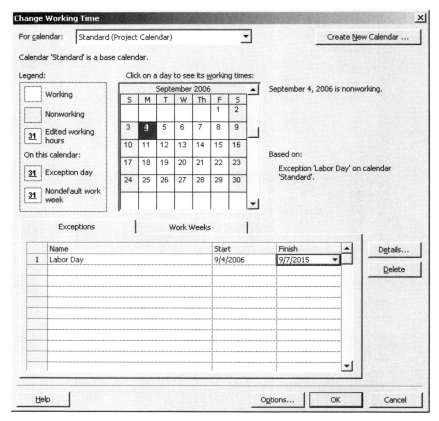

**Figure 1-5: Change Working Time dialog
with Labor Day holiday set**

Setting the Daily Working Schedule

After setting your company holidays, you should also establish your company's daily working schedule. By default, Microsoft Office Project 2007 assumes a daily working schedule of 8:00 AM – 5:00 PM with one hour off for lunch, Monday through Friday, with Saturday and Sunday as nonworking times. To set any other type of daily working schedule, such as 7:00 AM – 3:30 PM with a half-hour for lunch, you must complete the following steps:

1. In the Change Working Time dialog, click the *Work Weeks* tab and then click the *Details* button.

The software displays the Details dialog for the Default working schedule, as shown in Figure 1-6.

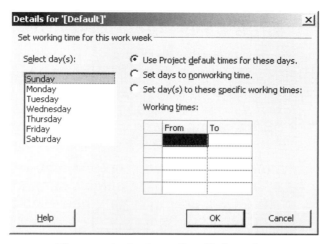

**Figure 1-6: Details dialog for
the Default working schedule**

2. In the Select Day(s) section, select and drag Monday through Friday in the list of days.

The software displays the default 8:00 AM – 5:00 PM working time in the *Working times* grid, shown in Figure 1-7.

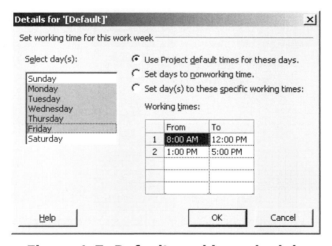

**Figure 1-7: Default working schedule
in the Details dialog**

3. Change the first *From* value to 7:00 AM or the appropriate value for your organization.

4. Change the second *From* value to 12:30 PM and change the second *To* value to 3:30 PM or the appropriate values for your organization.

5. Select any blank cell below the second line and then click the *OK* button.

6. Click the *OK* button in the Change Working Time dialog.

Creating a New Base Calendar

A Base Calendar is a master calendar that represents a unique working schedule for your company. Microsoft Office Project 2007 uses Base Calendars to schedule all work on a project and to set the working schedule for each resource. The software offers three predefined Base Calendars: a 24 Hours calendar, a Night Shift calendar, and a Standard calendar. The software sets Standard calendar as the Project Calendar for all new projects.

Because of unique scheduling needs in your project, you may need to create additional Base Calendars beyond the three default calendars that ship with Microsoft Office Project 2007. For example, you may need to schedule work to occur only on a weekend, or work to occur only on a 4-day working week (10 hours/day). For each of these scheduling needs, you must create a new Base Calendar. To create a new Base Calendar, complete the following steps:

1. Click Tools ➢ Change Working Time.

2. In the Change Working Time dialog, click the *Create New Calendar* button.

The software displays the Create New Base Calendar dialog shown in Figure 1-8.

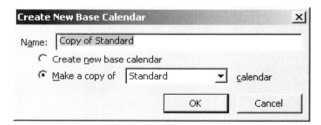

**Figure 1-8: Create New Base
Calendar dialog**

3. In the *Name* field, enter a name for your new base calendar.

4. To copy the existing schedule of company holidays, select the *Make a copy of Standard calendar* option. To create an entirely new calendar without company holidays, select the *Create new base calendar* option.

5. Click the *OK* button.

6. Set the working and nonworking schedule for the new calendar using the steps detailed in the previous two sections.

7. Click the *OK* button in the Change Working Time dialog.

Hands On Exercise

Exercise 1-2

Set the company holidays on the Standard calendar for the next 5 years beginning with New Year's Day of 2011.

1. Open the "Time Away Deployment 01" project file from your student folder.

2. Click Tools ➤ Change Working Time.

3. Select the Standard calendar and set the following company holidays:

   - New Years Day
   - Memorial Day – last Monday in May
   - Independence Day
   - Company picnic (afternoon off) – second Friday in August
   - Labor Day – first Monday in September
   - Thanksgiving – fourth Thursday in November
   - Friday following Thanksgiving
   - Christmas Day

Note: Set the date-driven holidays (New Year's, Independence Day, and Christmas) on the exact date they occur. Create additional exceptions when one of these holidays occurs on a weekend, such as setting December 31, 2010 as the New Year's Day 2011 holiday.

Exercise 1-3

You need a new base calendar called Weekend Work to schedule work that occurs only on a Saturday or Sunday. You need an additional base calendar called 4x10 Work for resources who work from Monday through Thursday only from 7:00 AM – 6:00 PM each day.

1. Create each of these base calendars, and then set the working schedule as specified.

2. Save but do not close your "Time Away Deployment 01" project.

Setting Project Options

Step 5, Setting project options unique to your project, is an essential step in defining a new project. Microsoft Office Project 2007 allows you to set two types of options:

- Options that control all project displays and behaviors.

- Options that govern the behavior and display of the active project only.

To set both types of options in Microsoft Office Project 2007, complete the following steps:

1. Click Tools ➢ Options.

The software displays the Options dialog shown in Figure 1-9.

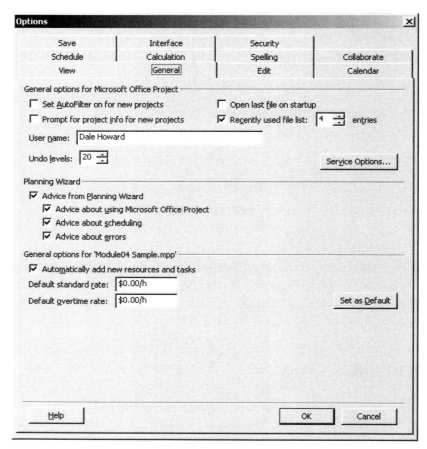

**Figure 1-9: Options dialog,
General page options**

2. Select your options settings on each page of the dialog and then click the *OK* button.

Pay close attention to the type of option that you set. If you set a project-specific option in one project and then open another project, the software will not display your project-specific option setting in the second project. The following subtopics list changes to the various pages for 2007.

 Because changes for both Project Professional and Project Standard editions appear below, Project Standard users may not see all of these.

Changes to the View Tab:

- The *View* tab now contains a new *Calendar type* pick list that allows you to leverage new support for Hijri and Thai Buddhist calendar types.

- In the Show section, the software allows you to deselect the option to display the new 3-D graphic bar styles on the Gantt chart. The option defaults to the selected state.

- The Currency Options section now includes a new *Currency* pick list allowing you to select a world currency from the list. Previous versions allowed you to select the symbol only.

Changes to the General Tab:

- In the General Options for Microsoft Office Project section, the *Show startup Task Pane* option no longer appears in this section. This relates to displaying the Project Guide, a feature that Microsoft is de-emphasizing in this version. Introduced in 2002, the Project Guide was not widely adopted by the user community. We expect this feature to fade away in future versions.

- A new *Undo levels* pick list allows you to set the number of undo levels for your copy of the software.

Multi-level undo is perhaps the most exciting and most anticipated new feature Microsoft added in Microsoft Office Project 2007. You can now set your software to support up to a maximum of 99 undo levels. This option is available in the *Undo levels* option on the *General* tab shown in Figure 1-9. This capability allows the project manager to make changes in order to perform "what if?" scenario planning, and then undo the changes before saving the project. By default, the system ships with this option set to 20 levels of undo. You can specify up to 99 levels of undo. Keep in mind that the higher you set this option, the more hard drive space the system requires to track and undo your actions.

If you click the *Set as default* button in a project-specific section of the Options dialog, Microsoft Office Project 2007 uses these settings **only in new projects**. The software does not update your settings in current projects.

 MSProjectExperts recommends that you **do not** make changes to any of the Options settings unless you are certain about the impact of the resulting changes. Because many of the Options settings are global in nature, changing a project Option could affect all of your projects.

Changes to the Spelling Tab:

- The calendar tab now contains a *More Spelling Options* button where four option checkboxes used to appear. Clicking this button takes you to a new Spelling Options dialog shown in Figure 1-10.

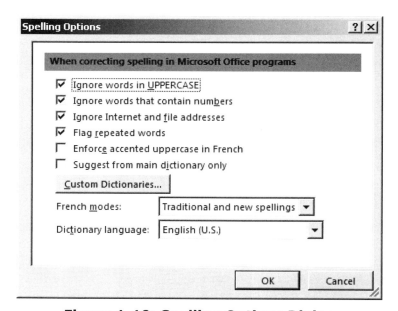

Figure 1-10: Spelling Options Dialog

- Notice the new options for 2007 include flagging repeated words, a button for defining custom dictionaries and new support for French language. You can now define your own dictionaries or select other dictionaries available on your system.

Changes to the Collaborate tab:

- The *Collaborate* tab is substantially different in 2007 from its appearance in 2002 and 2003. As these options specifically relate to using Project Professional with Project Server 2007, I do not cover these in this book.

Changes to the Save tab:

- Because Project 2007 no longer supports saving to ODBC databases, the changes to this tab are specific to this change. The *File Locations* section no longer contains file type specifics for Workgroup templates and ODBC Database selections.

- The option to expand timephased data in the database no longer appears in the lower section of the dialog.

Changes to the Interface tab:

- A new *User Interface* option allows you to deselect the default *Use internal IDs to match different-language or renamed Organizer items between projects* option. This new capability allows the system to recognize duplicate items unlike prior versions, which allowed duplications.

- The system no longer defaults to *Display Project Guide* option selected.

Changes to the Security tab:

- A new section containing a single option related to Project Server now appears below the Macro Security section.

- Because the file format changed with the 2007 release, a new *Legacy Formats* section provides options for setting the software behaviors when it encounters legacy file formats.

Hands On Exercise

Exercise 1-4

Set the project options for your Time Away Deployment project.

1. Return to your "Time Away Deployment 01" project file.
2. Click Tools ➢ Options.
3. Set the options recommended by MSProjectExperts as detailed on the previous four pages.
4. Click the *OK* button.
5. Save and close the "Time Away Deployment 01" project file.

Module 02

What's New Task Planning

Learning Objectives

After completing this module, you will be able to:

- Understand change highlighting
- Use cell background formatting to display tasks of interest
- Use Multi-Level Undo
- Understand task drivers

Understanding Change Highlighting

Microsoft Office Project 2007 includes a much awaited new feature; it is the first version of the software that immediately shows you the schedule changes while you manipulate the project schedule. This applies when you make manual changes to the project or when you run a VBA macro that changes the schedule. When you make a change anywhere in a Microsoft Office Project 2007 schedule, the software uses Change Highlighting to graphically show you all tasks impacted by the change. This behavior begins the moment you enter the first task in the project and continues until you complete the project.

After you define your project, the planning process begins. The first step in the planning process is task planning. You can create a task list, or work breakdown structure (WBS), in Microsoft Office Project 2007 by typing the list manually or by using a template. Change Highlighting begins the moment you start entering data in any task, resource, or assignment view screen. The system shows you the impact of each change by highlighting all tasks affected by each change.

For example, if you change the Duration of the first task in a chain of linked tasks, the software formats the background color of the Duration, Start, or Finish column for every task that follows in the chain. If the change in this work path impacts additional downstream tasks, these are highlighted as well. Figure 2-1 shows a project before I make revisions to the schedule. Figure 2-2 shows the same project after I change the Duration of Task C. Notice how Microsoft Office Project 2007 changes the cell formatting color for the *Duration* and *Finish* fields on Task C, and changes the cell formatting color to the *Start* and/or *Finish* columns of each impacted task and summary task, including the Project Summary Task.

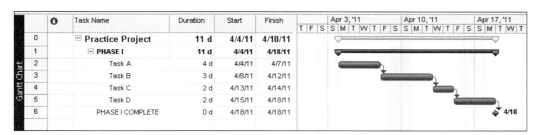

**Figure 2-1: Project before
schedule changes**

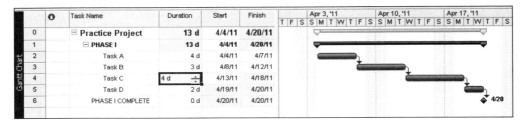

**Figure 2-2: Project after
making schedule changes**

 To change the cell background color used to indicate impacted tasks, click Format ➤ Text Styles, click the *Background Color* pick list and select a different color.

 To disable Change Highlighting, click View ➤ Hide Change Highlighting or click the *Hide Change Highlighting* button on the *Standard* toolbar.

If you find the change highlighting distracting while you build your initial schedule, you should turn off the feature until you complete your initial build. This new feature, combined with multi-level undo, provides the Project Manager with the additional business value of "What If?" scenario-planning. When you enter one set of possible project changes, this feature enables you to see all the downstream consequences for the project schedule related to that change. If you want, you may undo that first set of changes and try another and then see the "ripple effect" on the schedule for the second scenario.

Hands On Exercise

Exercise 2-1

Use Change Formatting while doing Duration planning in the Time Away Deployment project.

1. Open the "Time Away Deployment 02" project file from your student folder.

2. Observe the Change Formatting as you enter the following Duration values on tasks in the Testing phase of the project:

Install TimeAway Clients	7d
Verify Connectivity	5d
Resolve Connectivity Errors	4d

3. Observe the Change Formatting as you enter the following Duration values on tasks in the Training phase of the project:

Conduct Skills Assessment	7d
Create Training Schedule	6d

4. Save but do not close your "Time Away Deployment 02" project file.

Adding Cell Background Formatting

In Microsoft Office Project 2007, you can use a new feature called cell background formatting to easily identify tasks of interest, such as project milestones or slipping tasks, as well as to document extra information. This new feature is similar to the cell background formatting feature in Microsoft Office Excel 2007. You can manually set cell background formatting on one or more tasks, or you can set it automatically using a Filter or a VBA macro. To manually set cell background formatting on any task, complete the following steps:

1. Click the ID number for the task to select the entire task.

2. Click Format ➢ Font.

The system opens the Font dialog as shown in Figure 2-3.

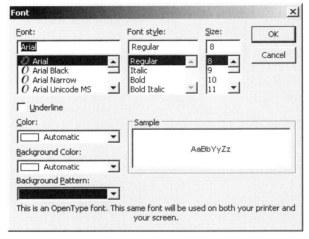

Figure 2-3: Font dialog

3. Click the *Background Color* pick list and select the color of your background formatting.

4. Click the *Background Pattern* pick list and select a pattern for the background color, if necessary.

5. Click the *Color* pick list and select an alternate color for the font, if necessary.

6. Click the *OK* button

In Figure 2-4, notice that I selected Yellow for the *Background Color* and Solid for the *Background Pattern*. Figure 2-5 shows the resulting background cell formatting on Task C.

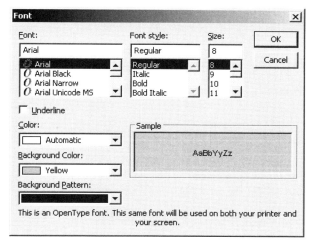

**Figure 2-4: Cell background
formatting applied**

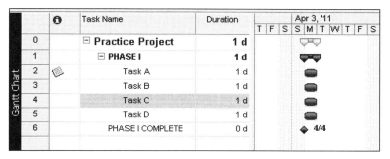

**Figure 2-5: Cell background
formatting on Task C**

 Cell background formatting, like text formatting in Microsoft Office Project 2007, is an attribute of the View in which you apply the formatting. When you apply cell background formatting to a task, Microsoft Office Project 2007 applies formatting to the task for all Tables **in the current View only**.

For example, if you apply the Aqua color to a task displayed in the Gantt Chart view, the software applies the background formatting to the task in every Task table you apply in the Gantt Chart view (such as the Cost and Work tables).

However, if you display the Tracking Gantt view, the system does not apply any cell formatting to the task in this View. This means that you can apply cell background formatting to different tasks in different Views.

Hands On Exercise

Exercise 2-2

Apply cell background formatting to each of the Milestone tasks in the TimeAway Deployment project.

1. Return to your "Time Away Deployment 02" project file.

2. Using the *Control* key, select the ID numbers for **all** of the Milestone tasks in the project.

3. Click Format ➢ Font.

4. Set the *Background Color* field value to Yellow and the *Background Color* field value to Solid and then click the *OK* button.

5. Save but do not close your "Time Away Deployment 02" project file.

Using Multi-Level Undo

Multi-level undo is perhaps the most useful new feature in Project 2007, and certainly the most anticipated! In all previous versions of the software, you could **only** undo the last action you performed. Now, the software allows you to undo as many of your previous actions as you selected for your undo level in the options settings in Module 2. These are displayed in the drop-down list when you click the pick list arrow next to the *Undo* or *Redo* buttons. Figure 2-6 shows an example of the drop-down list that displays when you click the Undo pick list.

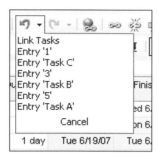

**Figure 2-6: Drop-down list of actions
for the Undo button**

The *Undo* pick list shows your actions from the most recent at the top with each prior action listed below it in order. You can select as many levels to undo as you want by floating your mouse pointer down the list. This avoids the need to repeatedly click the *Undo* button.

 Just as in Microsoft Office Word 2007 and Microsoft Office Excel 2007, the Multi-Level Undo feature allows you to undo previous actions sequentially, not selectively. That is, as you go down the *Undo* pick list, the software does not allow you to select certain actions to undo while skipping others.

Using the Task Drivers Feature

The Task Drivers feature is an exciting new addition to Microsoft Office Project 2007 that allows you to determine the task drivers for any task. Previous versions of the software required you to run a macro to determine this information as the Gantt Chart view, alone, does not provide the information required to determine what was driving the start date of any task. Simply put, a task driver is any factor that determines the start date of a task. Task drivers can include any of the following:

- Start No Earlier Than (SNET) constraints

- Predecessor tasks (including Lag time)

- Nonworking time on both the Project calendar and the personal calendars of resources assigned to the task

- Leveling delays caused by leveling resource overallocations

- An Actual Start date on the task

You can determine the task drivers for any task by completing the following steps:

1. Click Project ➤ Task Drivers or click the *Task Drivers* button 🔳 on the *Standard* toolbar.

2. Select the task for which you want to determine drivers.

The software displays the task drivers for the selected task in the Task Drivers sidepane, as shown in Figure 2-7. Notice that the Task Drivers sidepane shows that the task drivers on the selected task include a predecessor task as well as Gene Cain's and Amy McKay's working calendars.

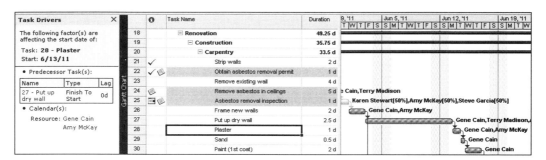

**Figure 2-7: Task Drivers for
the selected task**

3. To view the calendar for any resource assigned to the selected task, click the name of the resource in the Task Drivers sidepane.

For example, Figure 2-8 shows the calendar for Gene Cain. Notice that I scheduled him for a week of vacation from June 6-10, 2011. This period of nonworking time affects the Start and/or Finish dates of any task previously scheduled during that week.

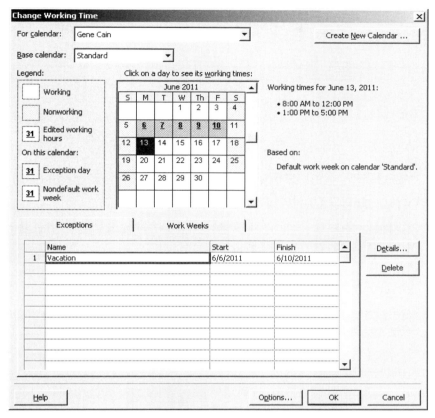

**Figure 2-8: Change Working Time
dialog for Gene Cain**

4. Close the Task Drivers sidepane when finished.

 This new feature in Microsoft Office Project 2007 enables the Project Manager to determine whether the Start date for a task is due to business constraints or to Critical Path constraints.

Hands On Exercise

Exercise 2-3

Determine task drivers for tasks in the Time Away Deployment project.

1. Return to your "Time Away Deployment 02" project file.

2. Click Project ➢ Task Drivers.

3. Select task ID #5, Perform Server Stress Test, and determine the task driver for this task.

4. Select task ID #9, Verify Connectivity, and determine the task driver for this task.

5. Select task ID #19, Conduct Skills Assessment, and determine the task driver for this task.

6. Select task ID #21, Provide Training, and determine the task driver for this task.

7. Save and close your "Time Away Deployment 02" project file.

Module 03

What's New Resource & Assignment Planning

Learning Objectives

After completing this module, you will be able to:

- Work with resource calendars
- Understand Cost resources
- Create Budget Cost resources and Expense Cost resources
- Assign Budget Cost resources and Expense Cost resources to a task
- Enter actuals on an Expense Cost resource

Entering Resource Information

As in previous versions of Microsoft Office Project, you enter project resources in two steps. The first step in the resource planning process is entering the basic resource information in the Resource Sheet view for each member of your project team, completing the information requested in each column. This step is unchanged in Microsoft Office Project 2007.

The second step is to enter custom information for each resource. Custom resource data includes information such as vacation time, alternate cost rates, or notes about the resource. Every aspect of modifying a resource calendar is different in Microsoft Office Project 2007 from prior versions. To enter this information, double-click the name of the resource and the system displays the Resource Information dialog shown in Figure 3-1.

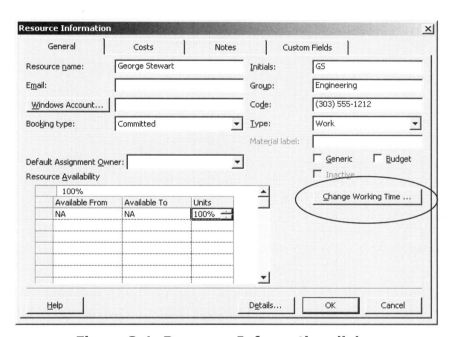

Figure 3-1: Resource Information dialog
General page

 You can also access the Resource Information dialog by doing either of the following:

- Click Project ➤ Resource Information.

- Click the *Resource Information* button 🖼 on the *Standard* toolbar.

One new feature in Microsoft Office Project 2007 is on the Resource Information dialog General page shown previously in Figure 3-1. In previous versions of Microsoft Office Project, the dialog contained a *Working Time* tab between the *General* and *Costs* tabs, which you used to access the resource calendar. Microsoft replaced this tab with the *Change Working Time* button, which I highlighted in the figure. Click this button to access the team member's personal calendar and to change the working schedule

Changing Working Time

Click the *Change Working Time* button to handle each of the following scenarios, using the new capabilities in Microsoft Office Project 2007 for modifying a resource's calendar:

- The resource works a schedule different from the schedule on the Standard calendar.

- To add nonworking time for the resource, such as vacation or planned sick leave.

- To make minor modifications to the resource working schedule, such as adding Saturday work for a specific period.

I discuss how to configure each of these schedule needs separately.

Setting an Alternate Working Schedule

If you want to create an alternate working schedule for a resource, and the schedule differs from the Standard calendar, there are two ways to accomplish this. To use the first method, you must create a custom Base calendar in the project. Refer to Module 02 for details on creating new Base calendars if necessary. After you create the custom Base Calendar, simply select that new calendar as the *Base Calendar* column for the selected resource(s) in the Resource Sheet view of the project.

If a Base Calendar with the schedule you wish does not already exist, you can specify the non-standard working schedule for the resource by completing the following steps:

1. Click the *Change Working Time* button on the *General* page of the Resource Information dialog. The software displays the Change Working Time dialog for the selected resource. For example, Figure 3-2 shows the Change Working Time dialog for George Stewart.

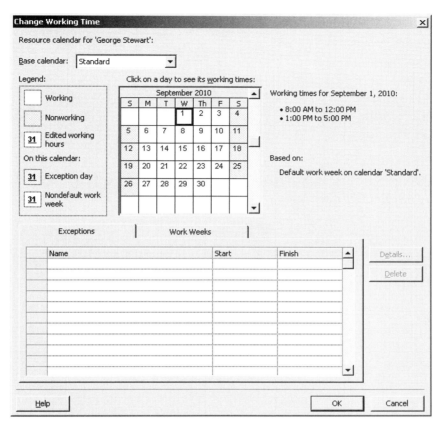

**Figure 3-2: Change Working Time
dialog, Exceptions tab**

2. Click the *Work Weeks* tab.

Figure 3-3 shows the *Work Weeks* tab in the Change Working Time dialog for George Stewart.

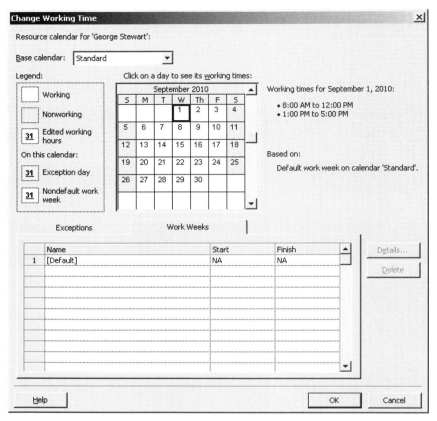

**Figure 3-3: Change Working Time
dialog, Work Weeks tab**

3. Select the [Default] item in the *Work Weeks* data grid and then click the *Details* button.

The software displays the Details dialog shown in Figure 3-4.

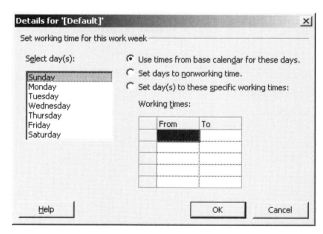

**Figure 3-4: Details dialog for
[Default] working schedule**

4. In the *Select day(s)* list, select the days you want to change.

5. Select one of the three working times options in the upper right corner of the dialog, such as the *Set days to nonworking time* option.

6. Enter the alternate working schedule in the *Working times* data grid.

Figures 3-5 and 3-6 show the Details dialog for a working schedule where the resource works 9 hours per day from Monday through Thursday, and 4 hours per day on Friday.

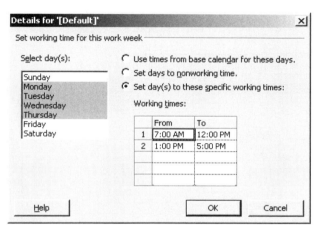

**Figure 3-5: Details dialog shows
Monday through Thursday
working schedule selected**

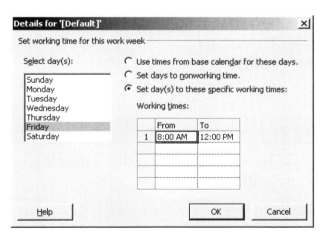

**Figure 3-6: Details dialog shows
Friday working schedule**

7. Click the *OK* button to close the Details dialog.

Figure 3-7 shows the Change Working Time dialog with the new alternate working schedule for George Stewart.

37

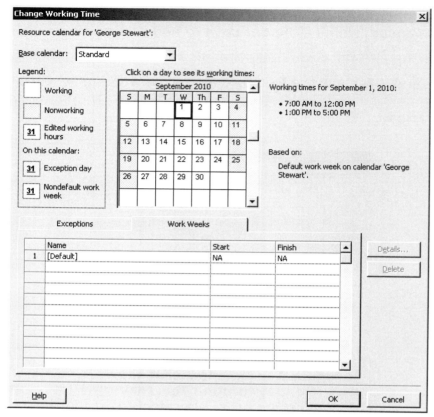

**Figure 3-7: Change Working Time dialog
with alternate working schedule**

Entering Nonworking Time

Microsoft Office Project 2007 allows you to enter nonworking time, such as vacations and sick leave, for each individual resource. To perform either of these actions, click the *Change Working Time* button on the General page. To enter nonworking time for the resource, complete the following steps:

1. Click the *Change Working Time* button on the General page of the Resource Information dialog.

2. Click the *Exceptions* tab.

Figure 3-8 shows the *Exceptions* tab of the Change Working Time dialog.

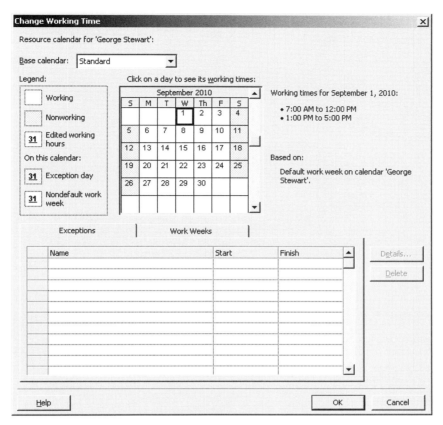

**Figure 3-8: Change Working Time
dialog, Exceptions tab**

3. In the calendar object at the top of the page, select the days you want to set as nonworking time.

4. In the first blank line of *Name* column, enter a name for the nonworking time instance, such as Vacation.

5. Press the Right-Arrow key.

The software automatically sets the selected period as nonworking time, such as the vacation time for George Stewart shown in Figure 3-9.

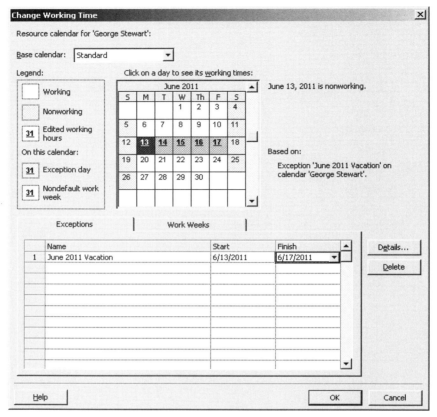

**Figure 3-9: Nonworking time
in June 2011 for George Stewart**

Setting Working Schedule Changes

To set a change to the regular working schedule for the resource, such as when you might ask a resource to extend their workweek for a specified period, complete the following steps:

1. Click the *Change Working Time* button on the General page of the Resource Information dialog.

2. Click the *Work Weeks* tab.

3. In the first blank line of the *Name* column, enter a name for the schedule change and then press the Right-Arrow key.

4. Enter the starting date of the schedule change in the *Start* field and enter the ending date in the *Finish* field.

For example, Figure 3-10 shows an extended working schedule change for George Stewart during the month of August 2011 only.

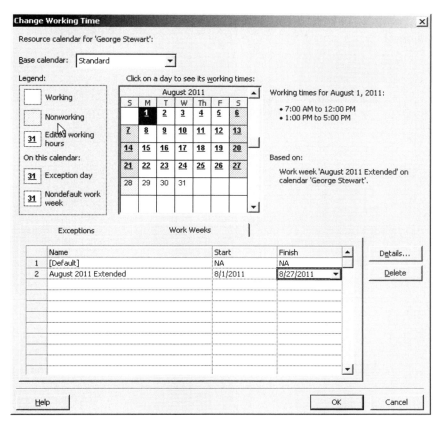

**Figure 3-10: Working schedule change
for August 2011 only**

5. Click the *Details* button. The software displays the Details dialog shown in Figure 3-11.

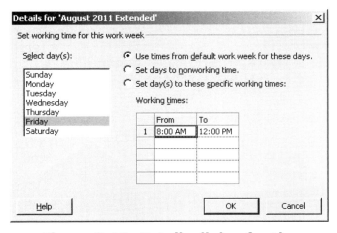

**Figure 3-11: Details dialog for the
August 2011 schedule change**

5. Enter the working change for each day of the week in the selected period.

Figures 3-12 and 3-13 show that George Stewart must work 9 hours each Friday and 5 hours each Saturday during August 2011 only.

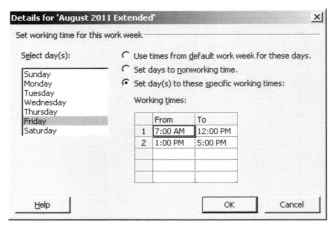

**Figure 3-12: Details dialog
shows Friday schedule change**

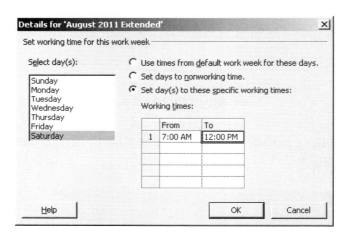

**Figure 3-13: Details dialog shows
Saturday schedule change**

6. Click the *OK* button to close the Details dialog.

Figure 3-14 shows the Change Working Time dialog with the August 2011 schedule change for George Stewart.

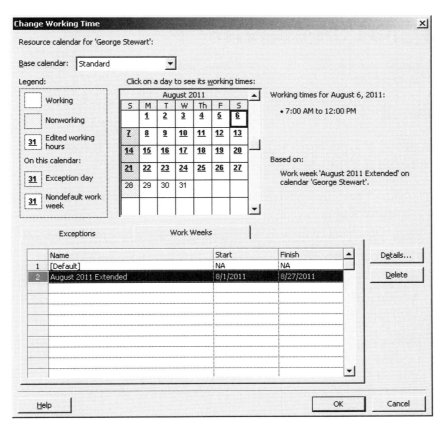

**Figure 3-14: Change Working Time dialog
with August 2011 schedule change**

Hands On Exercise

Exercise 3-1

Enter general and working schedule information for selected members of the project team in the Time Away Deployment.

1. Open the "Time Away Deployment 03" project file from your student folder.

2. Set an exception for Mickey Cobb to document March 14-18, 2011 as vacation.

3. Modify the working schedule for Jeff Holly to work **Monday through Saturday** from 8:00 AM – 5:00 PM during the month of April 2011 only.

4. Save and close your "Time Away Deployment 03" project file.

Using Cost Resources

Previous versions of Microsoft Office Project provided you with only two types of resources: Work and Material. Microsoft Office Project 2007 now offers you a third type of resource, the Cost Resource. You can use Cost resources to support several situations:

- You need to connect data in your project to a third-party financial system.

- Your organization specifies a budget for each project and you enter actual project costs manually in the Microsoft Office Project 2007 plan.

- You need to add extra costs to tasks that you cannot track by using the Fixed Cost feature for tasks.

Microsoft Office Project 2007 provides you with two types of Cost resources: Budget Cost resources and Expense Cost resources, each of which I explain below. To use Cost resources effectively you should create at least one Budget Cost resource and a corresponding Expense Cost resource in the Resource Sheet view. You should also set the Standard Rate, Overtime Rate, and Cost/Use Rate to $0.00 for all human, Material and Generic resources in the Resource Sheet. It is important that you set the cost rates for all non-Cost resources to $0.00 because using Cost resources assumes that you manually enter your project budget and actual costs in the project.

Creating a Budget Cost Resource

To create a Budget Cost resource, complete the following steps:

1. Click View ➢ Resource Sheet.

2. Enter the name of your Budget Cost resource.

3. Click the Type pick list and select the Cost item from the list.

Notice in Figure 3-15 that I am creating a Budget Cost resource named Project Budget.

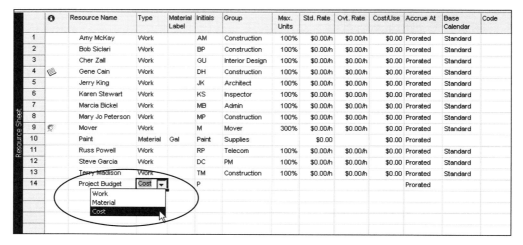

**Figure 3-15: Create Budget
Cost resource**

4. Enter additional information for the Budget Cost resource in the *Initials, Group, Accrue At*, and *Code* fields, as needed.

5. Double-click the name of the Budget Cost resource.

6. On the General page of the Resource Information dialog, select the *Budget* option shown in Figure 3-16.

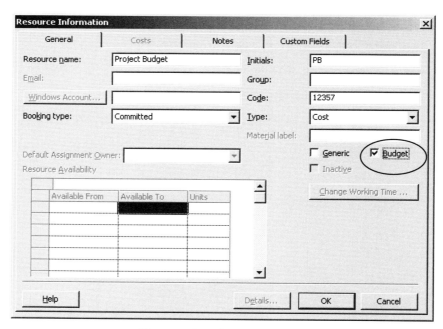

**Figure 3-16: Create an
Expense Cost resource**

7. Click the *OK* button.

Figure 3-17 shows my completed Project Budget Cost resource.

Figure 3-17: Completed
Budget Cost resource

Cost resources differ from Work resources and Material resources in that Cost resources do not cost a project on a task-by-task or a resource-by-resource basis.

Creating an Expense Cost Resource

To create an Expense Cost resource, complete the following steps:

1. Click View ➢ Resource Sheet.

2. Enter the name of your Expense Cost resource.

3. Click the *Type* pick list and select the *Cost* item from the list.

4. Enter additional information for the Expense Cost resource in the *Initials, Group, Accrue At*, and *Code* fields, as needed.

Figure 3-18 shows my new Expense Cost resource named Project Expense.

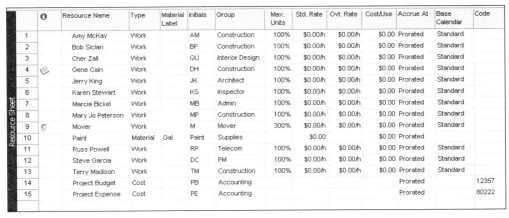

Figure 3-18: Completed
Budget Cost resource

47

Assigning a Budget Cost Resource to a Task

When you use a Budget Cost resource Microsoft Office Project 2007 allows you to assign the resource only to the Project Summary Task (Row 0). This allows you to set a budget for the project as a whole, but does not allow you to set a budget on Phases, Deliverables, or individual tasks. To set a budget for your project, complete the following steps:

- Click View ➢ Task Usage and then select the Project Summary Task (Row 0).

- Click the *Assign Resources* button on the *Standard* toolbar, select your Budget Cost resource, and then click the *Assign* button.

- Click the *Close* button.

 If you have not previously displayed the project summary task (Row 0), click Tools ➢ Options and select the View tab. In the *Outline Options For* section at the bottom of the *Dialog* tab, select the *Show Project Summary Task* option.

Figure 3-19 shows that I assigned my Project Budget resource to the Project Summary Task.

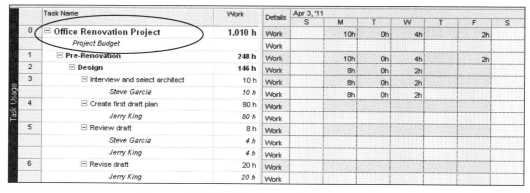

**Figure 3-19: Budget Cost resource
assigned to the Project Summary Task**

1. Click View ➢ Table ➢ Cost to apply the Cost table.

2. Right-click on the Fixed Cost column header, click the *Insert Column* item in the shortcut menu, and then insert the *Budget Cost* column.

3. Right-click anywhere in the timephased grid (yellow timesheet on the right) and then click the *Detail Styles* item in the shortcut menu.

4. In the Detail Styles dialog, add the *Budget Cost* field to the list of fields on the right and then click the *OK* button.

Figure 3-20 shows the Detail Styles dialog with the *Budget Cost* field added. Figure 3-21 shows the Task Usage view with the *Budget Cost* field displayed in the Cost table and in the timephased grid.

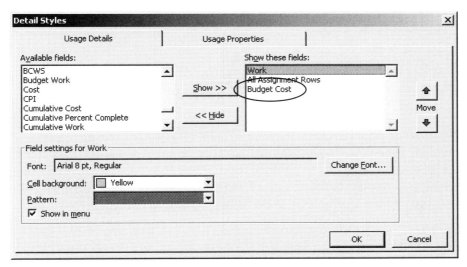

**Figure 3-20: Detail Styles dialog
with Budget Cost field added**

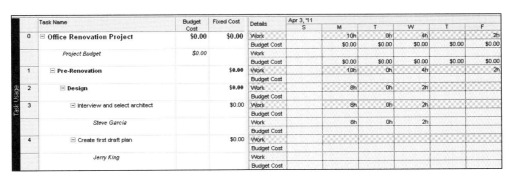

**Figure 3-21: Task Usage view
prepared to enter project budget**

5. In the Budget Cost cell for the Budget Cost resource assigned to the Project Summary task, enter your planned budget for the entire project and then press the *Enter* key.

Figure 3-22 shows the Budget Cost value for my Project Budget resource.

49

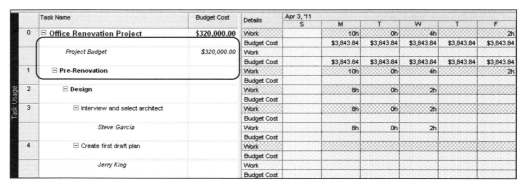

**Figure 3-22: Budget Cost
for entire project**

If you set the *Accrue At* field value to *Prorated* for the Budget Cost resource, Microsoft Office Project 2007 distributes the Budget Cost evenly across the Duration of the task as shown in the timephased grid in Figure 3-22. If you wish to distribute the Budget Cost information in another manner, such as on a monthly basis, then complete the following steps:

- Click the *Zoom Out* or *Zoom In* buttons on the *Standard* toolbar to zoom the timescale to the level of detail at which to set the Budget Cost.

- In the timephased grid, enter your anticipated Budget Cost values in the Budget Cost cells for your Budget Cost resource assignment.

In Figure 3-23, notice that I entered my project budget information on a monthly basis, roughly timephased to correspond with the planned Work hours for each month.

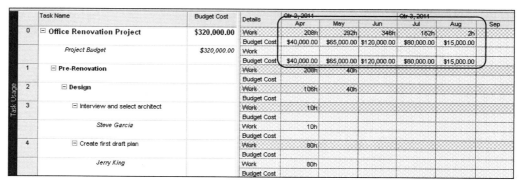

**Figure 3-23: Project Budget information
entered in timephased grid**

In addition to the *Budget Cost* field, Microsoft Office Project 2007 includes an additional budget field called Budget Work. This allows you to set a budget for working hours for your project in addition to a cost budget.

Assigning an Expense Cost Resource to a Task

After you enter your project budget using a Budget Cost resource, you need to assign Expense Cost resources to your project so that you can track actual project expenses. Microsoft Office Project 2007 allows you to assign Expense Cost resources to any type of task in the project including summary tasks, subtasks, and Milestone tasks. The software does not allow you to assign an Expense Cost resource to the Project Summary Task. To assign an Expense Cost resource to tasks in your project, complete the following steps:

1. Click View ➤ Gantt Chart.

2. Select one or more summary tasks, subtasks, or Milestone tasks in the project.

3. Click the *Assign Resources* button on the *Standard* toolbar, select your Expense Cost resource, and then click the *Assign* button.

4. Continue selecting tasks and assigning the Expense Cost resource until you finish.

5. Click the *Close* button.

To enter actual project costs in your project, complete the following steps:

1. Click View ➤ Task Usage.

Figure 3-24 shows that I assigned the Project Expense resource to each of the first-level summary tasks in my project. This is because I intend to track actual project expenses only at the Phase level in the project and each first-level summary task is a Phase.

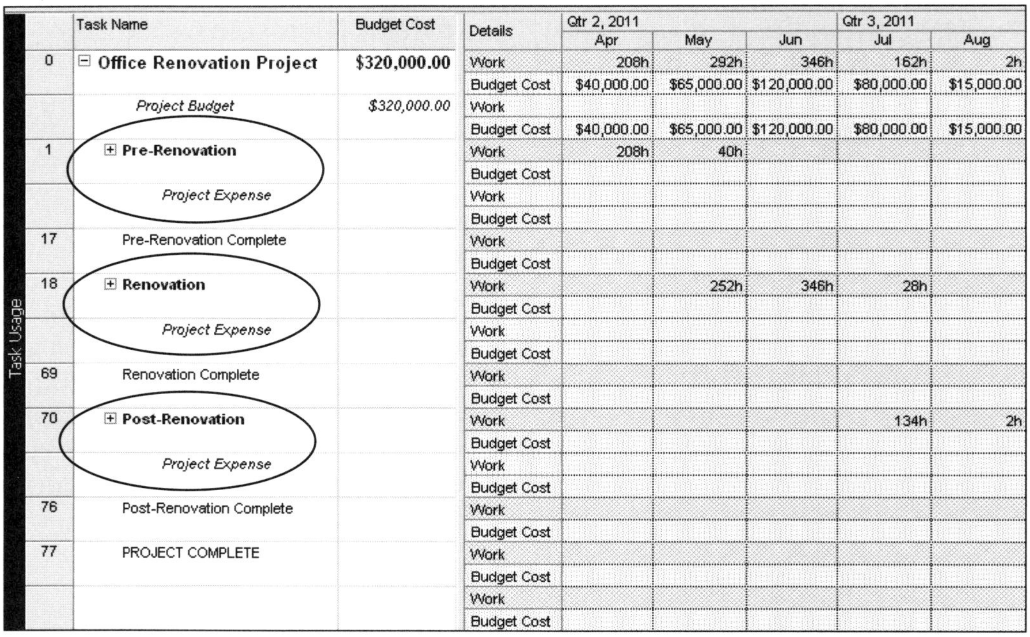

**Figure 3-24: Project Expense resource
assigned to summary task**

2. Pull the split bar to the right so that you can locate the *Actual Cost* column in the Cost table.

3. Select the *Actual Cost* column and drag it to the right of the *Budget Cost* column.

4. Right-click anywhere in the timephased grid (yellow timesheet on the right), select the Actual Cost item and deselect the Work item from the shortcut menu.

Figure 3-25 shows the Task Usage view set up to enter Actual Cost values for each Phase in my project.

	Task Name	Budget Cost	Actual	Details	Qtr 2, 2011			Qtr 3, 2011	
					Apr	May	Jun	Jul	Aug
0	⊟ Office Renovation Project	$320,000.00	$0.00	Budget Cost	$40,000.00	$65,000.00	$120,000.00	$80,000.00	$15,000.00
				Act. Cost	$0.00	$0.00			
	Project Budget	*$320,000.00*		Budget Cost	$40,000.00	$65,000.00	$120,000.00	$80,000.00	$15,000.00
				Act. Cost					
1	⊞ Pre-Renovation		$0.00	Budget Cost					
				Act. Cost	$0.00	$0.00			
	Project Expense		*$0.00*	Budget Cost					
				Act. Cost					
17	Pre-Renovation Complete		$0.00	Budget Cost					
				Act. Cost					
18	⊞ Renovation		$0.00	Budget Cost					
				Act. Cost		$0.00			
	Project Expense		*$0.00*	Budget Cost					
				Act. Cost					
69	Renovation Complete		$0.00	Budget Cost					
				Act. Cost					
70	⊞ Post-Renovation		$0.00	Budget Cost					
				Act. Cost					
	Project Expense		*$0.00*	Budget Cost					
				Act. Cost					
76	Post-Renovation Complete		$0.00	Budget Cost					
				Act. Cost					
77	PROJECT COMPLETE		$0.00	Budget Cost					
				Act. Cost					
				Budget Cost					
				Act. Cost					

**Figure 3-25: Task Usage view
prepared to track Actual Costs**

Entering Actuals for Expense Cost Resources

To enter Actual Cost information in your project, enter the cost in the *Actual Cost* column for the Expense Cost resource assignment to expense. Microsoft Office Project 2007 distributes the Actual Cost evenly across the Duration of the task in the timephased grid. If you want to reallocate the Actual Cost, type the Actual Cost values in the timephased grid. Figure 3-26 shows the Task Usage view after I entered $60,000 of Actual Cost for the Project Expense cost resource assigned to the Pre-Renovation phase. Figure 3-27 shows the Task Usage view after I split the $60,000 of Actual Cost in the timephased grid to $42,000 in April 2011 and $18,000 in May 2011.

When you baseline your project, Microsoft Office Project 2007 saves the Budget Cost value in the *Baseline Budget Cost* field and saves the Budget Work value in the *Baseline Budget Work* field.

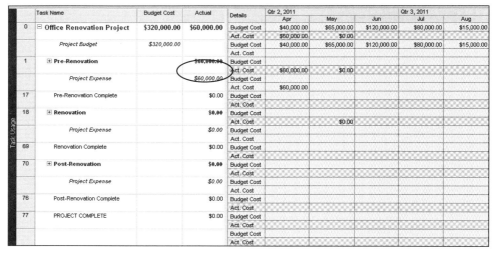

**Figure 3-26: Task Usage view
after entering $60,000 Actual Cost**

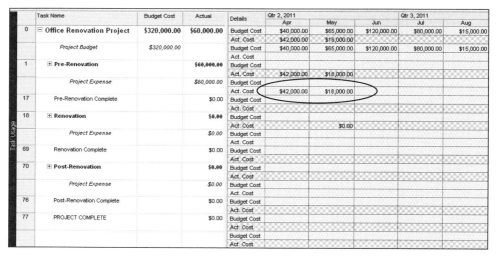

**Figure 3-27: Task Usage view after
redistributing $60,000 Actual Cost**

 If you specify a Budget Work estimate in addition to a Budget Cost estimate for your project, you can track Actual Work in the same manner as you track Actual Cost. Simply add the *Actual Work* field to the right of the *Actual Cost* field in the Table and add the Actual Work details in the timephased grid.

Hands On Exercise

Exercise 3-2

Create a custom Table to track your project Budget and Actual Costs using Cost resources.

1. Open the "Cost Resources" project file from your student folder.

2. Click View ➢ Table ➢ More Tables.

3. In the More Tables dialog, copy the Cost table and name it _Budget Tracking.

4. Select the *Show in menu* option and then include only the following fields in the Table definition:

Field Name	Align Data	Width	Title	Align Title
ID	Center	6		Center
Indicators	Left	8		Left
Name	Left	44	Task Name	Left
Budget Cost	Right	14		Center
Actual Cost	Right	14		Center

5. Click the *OK* button and then click the *Close* button.

6. Save but do not close your "Cost Resources" project file.

Hands On Exercise

Exercise 3-3

Create a custom View to track your project Budget and Actual Costs using Cost resources.

1. Return to your "Cost Resources" project file.

2. Click View ➤ More Views.

3. In the More Views dialog, copy the Task Usage view and name it _Budget Tracking_.

4. Select the following options in your new _Budget Tracking view definition:

Table	_Budget Tracking
Group	No Group
Filter	All Tasks
Highlight filter	Not selected
Show in menu	Selected

5. Click the *OK* button and then click the *Apply* button.

Your initial _Budget Tracking view should appear as shown in Figure 3-28.

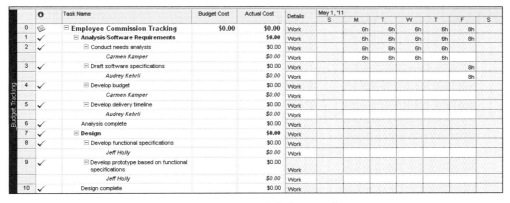

**Figure 3-28: Initial _Budget
Tracking view**

6. Right-click anywhere in the timephased grid (yellow timesheet on the right) and click *Detail Styles* on the shortcut menu.

7. In the Detail Styles dialog, add the *Budget Cost* and *Actual Cost* fields to the list on the right, remove the *Work* field, and then click the *OK* button.

Your completed _Budget Tracking view should appear as shown in Figure 3-29.

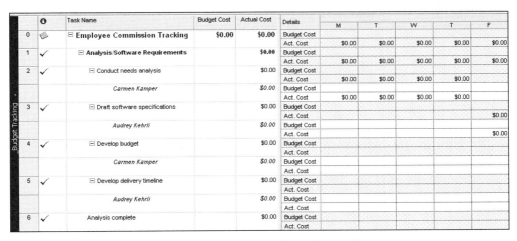

**Figure 3-29: Completed _Budget
Tracking view**

8. Save but do not close your "Cost Resources" project file.

Hands On Exercise

Exercise 3-4

Create Cost resources to track your project Budget and Actual Costs.

1. Return to your "Cost Resources" project file.
2. Click View ➢ Resource Sheet.
3. Create a Cost resource named Acct Budget.
4. Double-click the Acct Budget resource, select the *Budget* option in the Resource Information dialog, and then click the *OK* button.
5. Create a Cost resource named Acct Expenses.
6. Set the following additional information for each Cost resource:

Name	Initials	Group	Accrue At	Code
Acct Budget	AB	Accounting	Prorated	999
Acct Expenses	AE	Accounting	Prorated	999

7. Save but do not close your "Cost Resources" project file.

Exercise 3-5

Assign your new Cost resources to tasks in your project.

1. Return to your "Cost Resources" project file.
2. Click View ➢ _Budget Tracking to apply your new _Budget Tracking view.
3. Select the Project Summary Task (Row 0) and then click the *Assign Resources* button on the *Standard* toolbar.
4. In the Assign Resources dialog, select the Acct Budget resource and then click the *Assign* button.

5. Assign the Acct Expenses resource to the following first-level summary tasks and then close the Assign Resources dialog:

    -   Analysis/Software Requirements
    -   Design
    -   Development
    -   Testing

6. Click the *Show* button on the *Formatting* toolbar and select *Outline Level 1* from the pick list.

Your project should appear as shown in Figure 3-30.

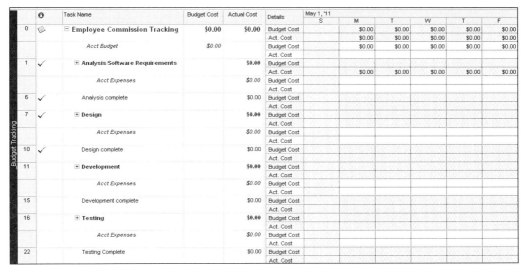

**Figure 3-30: Project with Cost
resources assigned to tasks**

7. Save but do not close your "Cost Resources" project file.

Hands On Exercise

Exercise 3-6

Set a budget for your project and enter Actual Cost for the first Phase of the project.

1. Return to your "Cost Resources" project file.

2. For the Acct Budget assigned to the Project Summary Task, enter $30,000 in the *Budget Cost* column.

3. Click the *Zoom Out* button on the *Standard* toolbar and zoom to *Quarters over Months*.

4. In the timephased grid (yellow timesheet on the right), enter the following Budget Cost values for the Acct Budget assignment on the Project Summary Task (Row 0):

Details	May	June	July
Budget Cost	$8,000	$13,000	$9,000

5. For the Acct Expenses resource assigned to the Analysis/Software Requirements task, enter $3,250 in the *Actual Work* column.

Your project should appear as shown in Figure 3-31.

	❶	Task Name	Budget Cost	Actual Cost	Details	Qtr 2, 2011			Qtr 3, 2011
						Apr	May	Jun	Jul
0	📝	⊟ Employee Commission Tracking	$30,000.00	$3,250.00	Budget Cost		$8,000.00	$13,000.00	$9,000.00
					Act. Cost		$3,250.00	$0.00	
		Acct Budget	$30,000.00		Budget Cost		$8,000.00	$13,000.00	$9,000.00
					Act. Cost				
1		⊞ Analysis/Software Requirements		$3,250.00	Budget Cost				
					Act. Cost		$3,250.00		
		Acct Expenses		$3,250.00	Budget Cost				
					Act. Cost		$3,250.00		
6	✓	Analysis complete		$0.00	Budget Cost				
					Act. Cost				
7	✓	⊞ Design		$0.00	Budget Cost				
					Act. Cost		$0.00	$0.00	
		Acct Expenses		$0.00	Budget Cost				
					Act. Cost				
10	✓	Design complete		$0.00	Budget Cost				
					Act. Cost				
11		⊞ Development		$0.00	Budget Cost				
					Act. Cost				
		Acct Expenses		$0.00	Budget Cost				
					Act. Cost				
15		Development complete		$0.00	Budget Cost				
					Act. Cost				
16		⊞ Testing		$0.00	Budget Cost				
					Act. Cost				
		Acct Expenses		$0.00	Budget Cost				
					Act. Cost				
22		Testing Complete		$0.00	Budget Cost				
					Act. Cost				

**Figure 3-31: Project after entering
Actual Work on the first Phase**

6. Click Tools ➢ Organizer and copy the new View and Table to your Global.mpt file.

7. Save and close your "Cost Resources" project file.

Module 04

What's New Project Reporting

Learning Objectives

After completing this module, you will be able to:

- Understand the new reporting features in Microsoft Office Project 2007, and which reporting features are unchanged
- View and modify default Visual Reports
- Create custom Visual Reports
- Create and manage Visual Report templates
- Use Cell Background Formatting for Critical Tasks

Using Project 2007 Visual Reports

Reporting has never been one of Project's strong points until the release of Microsoft Office Project 2007. With the introduction of Visual Reports in Microsoft Office Project 2007, you can now create much more robust reports on project data than ever before. During project execution, you typically must report project progress to one or more stakeholder groups. These include your project sponsor, your customer, your company executives, and even your project team. Microsoft Office Project 2007 offers you three ways to report project progress:

- Print default and custom Views.

- Print default and custom Reports.

- View and print Visual Reports.

All of the reports available in the first two categories remain completely unchanged in Microsoft Office Project 2007. Default and custom Views provide Reports that are screen prints, and default and custom Reports are all text-based. In the following sections you learn how to use Visual Reports in Project.

Creating Visual Reports

Visual Reports are an exciting new feature of Microsoft Office Project 2007 that allow you to see your project data in a PivotChart and PivotTable in Microsoft Office Excel 2007 or in a PivotDiagram in Microsoft Office Visio 2007. The software creates the Visual Report by building local OLAP (On Line Analytical Programming) cubes directly on your computer hard drive. These local OLAP cubes provide a multi-dimensional summary of task and resource data in your project.

Microsoft Office Project 2007 allows you to choose the fields to display in the Visual Report while viewing it and to make ad hoc modifications to the Visual Report without regenerating the underlying data. With this type of flexibility, Visual Reports offer you much greater flexibility than the default Reports that ship with the software.

Microsoft Office Project 2007 thus provides two new Reporting features: the capability of printing preformatted (default) Visual Reports, and the capability of creating custom Visual Reports to meet special stakeholder needs. You need only a basic knowledge of Microsoft Office Excel 2007 and Microsoft Office Visio 2007 to use the default Visual Reports. However, to create custom Visual Reports, you should have reasonable experience using Microsoft Office Excel 2007 PivotTables and Microsoft Office Visio 2007 PivotDiagrams.

To access Visual Reports, click Report ➢ Visual Reports. Microsoft Office Project 2007 displays the Visual Reports – Create Report dialog, shown in Figure 4-1.

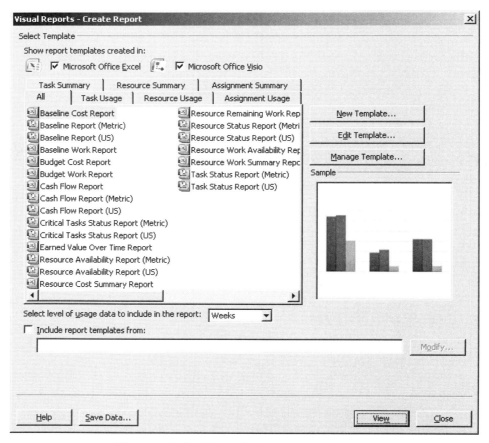

**Figure 4-1: Visual Reports - Create
Report dialog**

The Visual Reports – Create Report dialog provides you with six categories of default Visual Reports for both Microsoft Office Excel 2007 and Microsoft Office Visio 2007. The Task Usage, Resource Usage, and Assignment Usage categories display timephased task, resource, and assignment data respectively. The Task Summary, Resource Summary, and Assignment Summary categories display task, resource, and assignment data without timephased data. Tables 4-1 through 4-6 describe the default Visual Reports included in each category.

Task Usage		
Report Name	**Type**	**Description**
Cash Flow	Excel	Combination bar chart/line chart shows Cost and cumulative Cost over time.

Table 4-1: Task Usage Visual Reports

Resource Usage		
Report Name	**Type**	**Description**
Cash Flow	Visio	Diagram shows Cost and Actual Cost over time and broken down by resource type (Work, Material, and Cost). Diagram shows an orange triangle symbol
Resource Availability	Visio	Diagram shows Work and Remaining Availability for each resource, broken down by resource type (Work, Material, and Cost).
Resource Cost Summary	Excel	Pie chart shows project costs broken down by resource type (Work, Material, and Cost).
Resource Work Availability	Excel	Column chart shows total Work Availability, Work, and Remaining Availability for all resources.
Resource Work Summary	Excel	Column chart shows Work Availability, Work, Remaining Availability, and Actual Work for each resource individually.

Table 4-2: Resource Usage Visual Reports

Assignment Usage		
Report Name	**Type**	**Description**
Baseline Cost	Excel	Column chart shows Baseline Cost, Cost, and Actual Cost for all tasks with all first-level summary tasks collapsed.
Baseline	Visio	Diagram compares Work and Cost with Baseline Work and Baseline Cost over time for all tasks, with all first-level summary tasks collapsed. Diagram shows a red stoplight symbol when Work exceeds Baseline Work, and shows a yellow flag symbol when Cost exceeds Baseline Cost.
Baseline Work	Excel	Column chart shows Baseline Work, Work, and Actual Work for all tasks with all first-level summary tasks collapsed.
Budget Cost	Excel	Column chart shows Budget Cost, Baseline Cost, Cost, and Actual Cost over time.
Budget Work	Excel	Column chart shows Budget Work, Baseline Work, Work, and Actual Work over time.
Earned Value Over Time	Excel	Line chart shows Earned Value (EV), Planned Value (BCWP), and Actual Cost (ACWP) over time.

Table 4-3: Assignment Usage Visual Reports

 Warning: The Baseline report in Microsoft Office Visio 2007 is very difficult to read because of the black background. To change the background color click the *V-Background1* worksheet tab, click the background object to select it, and then click Format ➤ Fill.

Task Summary		
Report Name	**Type**	**Description**
Critical Tasks Status	Visio	Diagram shows Work, Remaining Work, and % Work Complete for both critical and non-critical tasks with all first-level summary tasks collapsed. Diagram shows a progress bar representing the % Work Complete for each task.

Table 4-4: Task Summary Visual Reports

Resource Summary		
Report Name	**Type**	**Description**
Resource Remaining Work	Excel	Stacked column chart shows Actual Work and Remaining Work for each resource individually.

Table 4-5: Resource Summary Visual Reports

Assignment Summary		
Report Name	**Type**	**Description**
Resource Status	Visio	Diagram shows Work and Cost for each resource with color shading in each box representing % Work Complete. White shading represents 100% Work complete, dark purple represents 0% Work complete, and light purple represents % Work Complete greater than 0% and less than 100%.
Task Status	Visio	Diagram displays Work and Cost for all tasks with all first-level summary tasks collapsed. Diagram shows an orange progress bar representing % Work Complete for each task and also shows a yellow "unhappy face" when Work exceeds Baseline Work. The system shows a yellow "neutral face" when Work is equal to or less than Baseline Work.

Table 4-6: Assignment Summary Visual Reports

 Each Microsoft Office Visio 2007 Visual Report is available in either a Metric version or US version. The versions refer to the measurement units applied to the horizontal and vertical Ruler bars. When you select the Metric version, the software applies the Millimeter measurement. When you select the US version, the software applies the Inches measurement.

Viewing a Visual Report

To view a Visual Report, complete the following steps:

1. Click Report ➢ Visual Reports.
2. In the Visual Reports – Create Report dialog, click the tab containing the Visual Report you want to view.
3. In your report section, select a Visual Report from the list.

4. Click the *Select level of usage data to include in this report* pick list and select the data granularity to include in the report, as shown in Figure 4-2.

 Microsoft Office Project 2007 generates the data in the local OLAP cubes using the granularity selected in step #4 above and then transfers the data to the Visual Report.

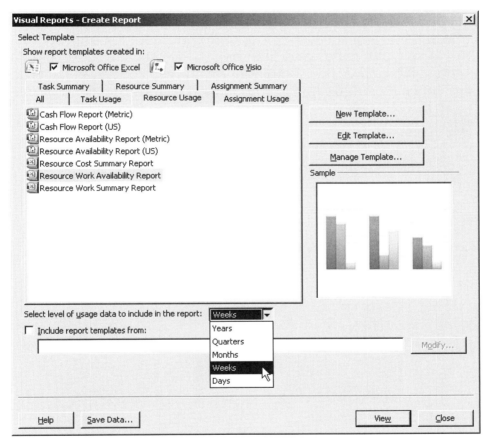

**Figure 4-2: Visual Reports – Create
Report dialog, select the granularity for
the Resource Work Availability Report**

Based on the size of your project, Microsoft Office Project 2007 sets a recommended value in the *Select level of usage data to include in this report* pick list. For most projects, the recommended value is Weeks. For very large projects, the recommended value might be Months, Quarters, or even Years.

5. Click the *View* button.

Microsoft Office Project 2007 displays a progress indicator at the bottom of the dialog in which it indicates that it is gathering data for the report, building the local OLAP cubes and then opens the Visual Report template for viewing. Figure 4-3 shows the completed Resource Work Availability Report in Microsoft Office Excel 2007. Note the legend at the top of the graph area.

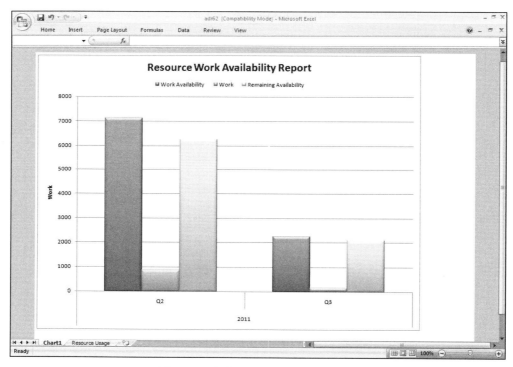

**Figure 4-3: Resource Work
Availability Visual Report**

6. Click the *Zoom Out* or *Zoom In* buttons in the lower right corner of the Excel 2007 window to set your desired level of zoom.

The system sets the default level of zoom for each Visual Report to 125%. Depending on your monitor size and screen resolution, you may need to zoom out for every Visual Report you view. Project 2007 is optimized for 1024 X 768 or higher resolution.

The Visual Report in Microsoft Office Excel 2007 consists of two parts: the graphical PivotChart and the PivotTable containing the underlying data. To view the PivotChart data, click either the *Task Usage* tab or the *Resource Usage* tab in the lower left corner of the application window. Figure 4-4 shows the PivotTable data on the Resource Usage worksheet for the Resource Work Availability Report.

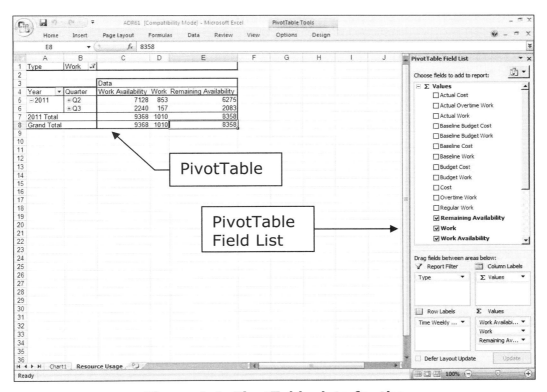

**Figure 4-4: PivotTable data for the
Resource Work Availability Report**

The PivotTable consists of several parts. The PivotTable itself is located in the upper left corner of the Excel worksheet shown in Figure 4-4 and includes drop areas for Rows, Columns, Filters and Totals. The PivotTable Field list is located in a pane on the right side of the screen.

Figure 4-5 shows the Task Status Visual Report in Microsoft Office Visio 2007. Because the default Zoom level is set to display the entire page, you will probably need to zoom in to see your Visual Report data clearly.

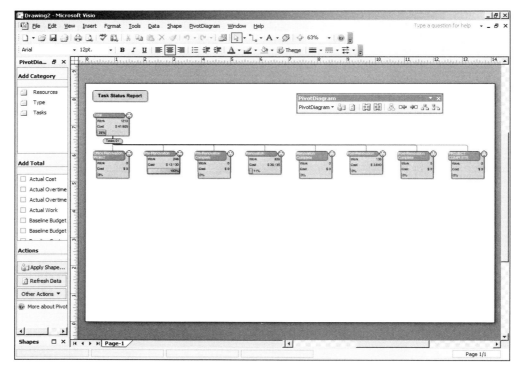

**Figure 4-5: Task Status
Visual Report**

Notice in Figure 4-5 that a Visual Report in Microsoft Office Visio 2007 consists of three parts: the PivotDiagram, the PivotDiagram sidepane on the left, and the floating PivotDiagram toolbar.

Hands On Exercise

Exercise 4-1

View Visual Reports in Microsoft Office Project 2007.

1. Return to your "Time Away Deployment 04" project file.

2. Click Report ➢ Visual Reports.

3. View and study the PivotChart and PivotTable, or PivotDiagram for each of the following Visual Reports:

   - Resource Cost Summary

   - Baseline Cost

   - Cash Flow (Visio)

4. Close and do not save the Microsoft Office Excel 2007 workbooks, but leave the Excel application running.

5. Close and do not save Microsoft Office Visio 2007 diagram, and close the Visio application.

6. Return to your Microsoft Office Project 2007 window and close the Visual Reports – Create Report dialog.

Customizing a Microsoft Office Excel 2007 Visual Report

You can customize any Microsoft Office Excel 2007 Visual Report by changing the PivotTable data on the Task Usage or Resource Usage page. For example, you can use any of the following methods to customize the PivotTable data in the Resource Work Availability Report:

- In the PivotTable click the *Expand* (+) or *Collapse* (-) buttons in the time section on the left side to show additional or fewer time periods. Notice in Figure 4-6 that I expanded the second quarter (Q2) to show Week 13 through Week 25. Microsoft Office Excel 2007 immediately updates the Visual Report based on the expanded second quarter information as shown in Figure 4-7.

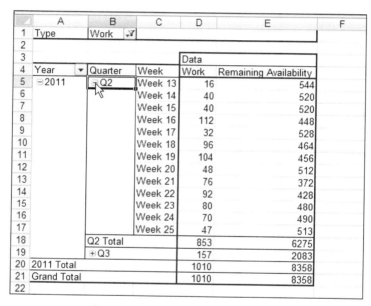

Figure 4-6: PivotTable with Q2 section expanded

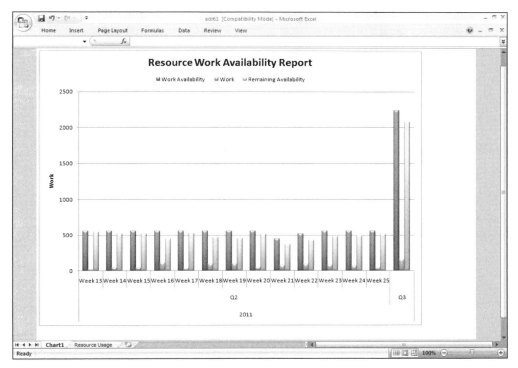

**Figure 4-7: Updated Resource
Work Availability Report**

- In the PivotTable Field List pane, select or deselect the fields you want to display. The software adds the newly selected field(s) to the appropriate drop area in the pane for Report Filter, Row Labels, Column Labels or Values.

- In the PivotTable Field List pane, drag and drop fields from the field list to the drop areas at the bottom of the pane or delete fields from any of the drop areas. Figure 4-8 shows that I removed the *Type* field from the Report Filter drop area and removed the *Work Availability* field from the Values drop area. Figure 4-9 shows the updated PivotChart.

**Figure 4-8: Drop Areas in the
PivotTable Field List pane**

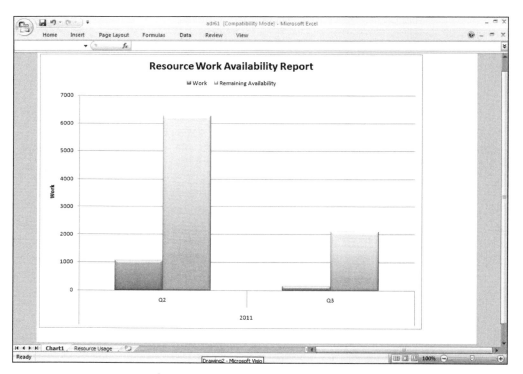

**Figure 4-9: Updated Resource
Work Availability Report**

You can also modify the PivotChart by selecting the Chart page and then by right clicking on the area of the chart you want to change. When I right click in the blank area of the PivotChart, Excel 2007 displays two formatting shortcut menus shown in Figure 4-10. From these two shortcut menus, you can use any of the available built-in formatting capabilities.

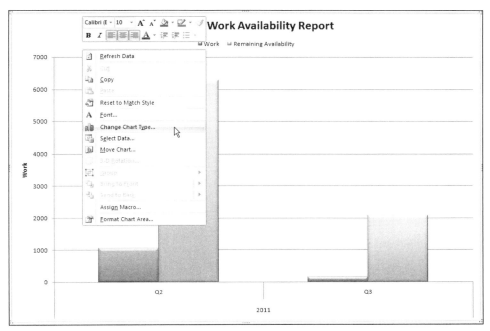

**Figure 4-10: Access shortcut menus
by right clicking in the PivotChart**

 Because this is not a course on Microsoft Office Excel 2007, I do not provide in-depth discussion of Excel chart formatting.

Figure 4-11 shows the PivotChart after I changed the *Chart Type* option to *Clustered Cylinder*.

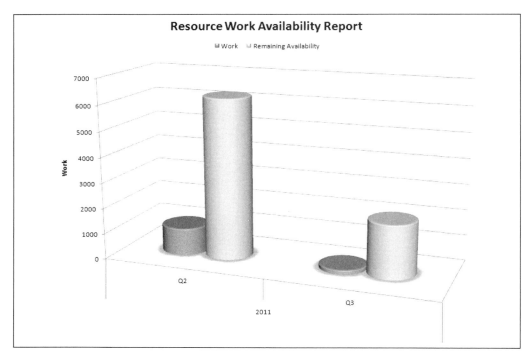

**Figure 4-11: PivotChart using
Clustered Cylinder chart type**

Within Microsoft Office Excel 2007, you can also do the following after viewing a Visual Report:

- Save the workbook by clicking the *Save* button.

- Print the workbook by clicking the *Office* button [image] in the upper left corner of the application window, and then click *Print* from the *Office* menu.

- Close the workbook without saving it and then exit the application.

Customizing a Microsoft Office Visio 2007 Visual Report

You can customize a Microsoft Office Visio 2007 Visual Report by using any of the following methods

- Select one or more objects in the PivotDiagram and then change the options in the sidepane or on the floating toolbar.

- Manually delete objects in the PivotDiagram.

- Change the layout of objects in the PivotDiagram.

Notice in the Task Status Visual Report, shown previously in Figure 4-5, that the Report displays only the first-level tasks representing the Phases in the project. In this Visual Report, I want to show the second-level summary tasks for the Renovation phase in order to view the Deliverables for that phase. To accomplish this, I must do the following:

1. Click the Renovation object to select it.

2. Hover the mouse pointer over the *Tasks* item in the Add Category section of the sidepane and then click the pick list arrow button as shown in Figure 4-12.

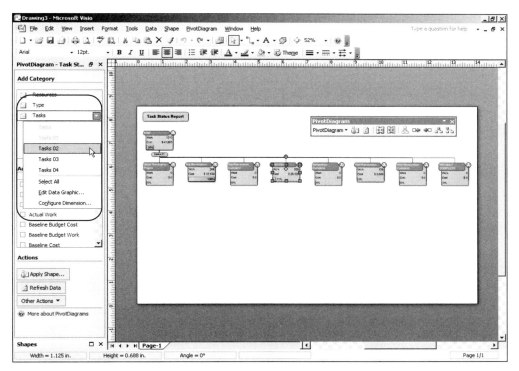

**Figure 4-12: Tasks menu in the
PivotDiagram sidepane**

3. Click the *Tasks 02* item on the pick list.

Figure 4-13 shows the Task Status Visual Report after adding the second-level summary tasks to the Report.

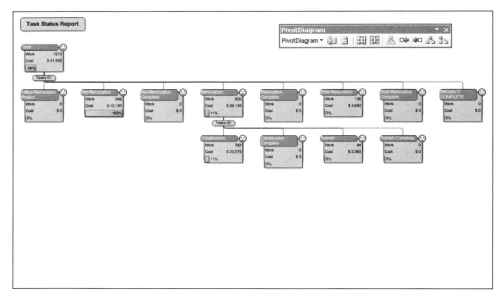

**Figure 4-13: Task Status Visual Report
with Deliverable tasks for the Renovation phase**

In the Task Status Visual Report shown in Figure 4-13, I want to remove the objects representing the Project Summary Task and all of the milestones. To delete an object, click the object to select it and then press the *Delete* key. Figure 4-14 shows my Task Status Visual Report after selecting and deleting these objects.

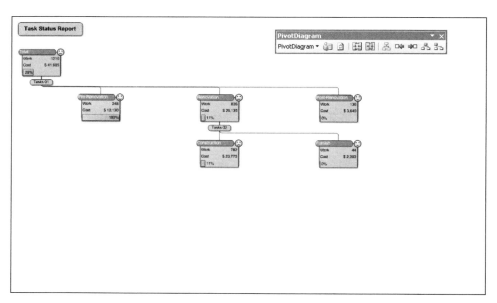

**Figure 4-14: Task Status Visual Report
after deleting four objects**

To change the layout of the objects, click the *Re-layout All* button on the floating *PivotDiagram* toolbar. You can also manually drag and drop objects anywhere on the PivotDiagram. Figure 4-15 shows the Task Status Visual Report zoomed to 100% after I changed the layout of the PivotDiagram using the *Re-layout All* button.

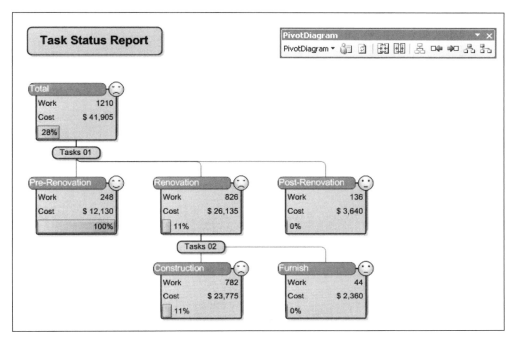

**Figure 4-15: Task Status Visual Report
after I change the layout**

> Because this is not a course on Microsoft Office Visio 2007, I do not provide in-depth discussion of PivotDiagram formatting.

You can also do the following after viewing a Visual Report within Microsoft Office Visio 2007:

- Save the Visual Report as a Drawing file.

- Print the Visual Report.

- Close the Visual Report without saving and then exit the application.

Hands On Exercise

Exercise 4-2

Customize the PivotTable in a Visual Report in Microsoft Office Excel 2007.

1. Return to your "Time Away Deployment 04" project file and then click Report ➢ Visual Reports.

2. In the Visual Reports – Create Report dialog, select the Baseline Work Report on the *Assignment Usage* tab and then click the *View* button.

3. In your Microsoft Office Excel 2007 window, click the *Assignment Usage* worksheet tab to view the PivotTable.

4. In the PivotTable, click the *Tasks* pick list arrow button to display the Select Field dialog shown in Figure 4-16.

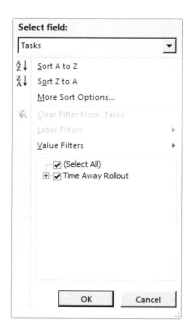

**Figure 4-16: Select Field
dialog in PivotTable**

5. In the Select Field dialog, expand the *Time Away Rollout* item to view summary tasks and milestones.

6. In the Select Field dialog, deselect the *(Select All)* option to deselect all tasks and then select only the following tasks:

- INSTALLATION
- TESTING
- TRAININING

7. Click the *OK* button.

8. Return to the PivotChart, zoom to 100%, and then study the differences.

Your Baseline Work Visual Report should appear as shown in Figure 4-17.

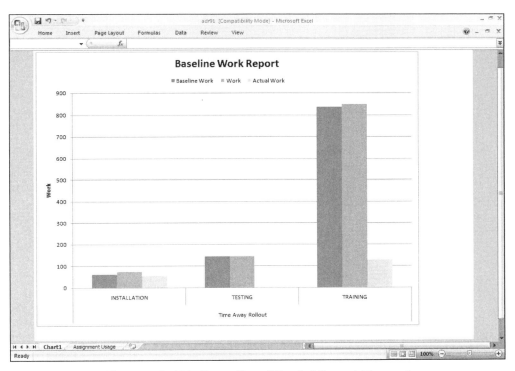

Figure 4-17: Baseline Work Visual Report
shows three Phases only

Hands On Exercise

Exercise 4-3

Customize the PivotChart in a Visual Report in Microsoft Office Excel 2007.

1. Return to your Baseline Work Visual Report in Microsoft Office Excel 2007, if necessary.

2. Click anywhere outside of the Chart area in the PivotChart and then close the *PivotTable Field List* sidepane on the right side of the screen.

3. Click the *Design* menu to display the ribbon menu.

4. Click the *Change Chart Type* button to display the Change Chart Type dialog.

5. Select the *Clustered Pyramid* option (second icon in the third row of the Column charts) and then click the *OK* button.

Your PivotChart should appear as shown in Figure 4-18.

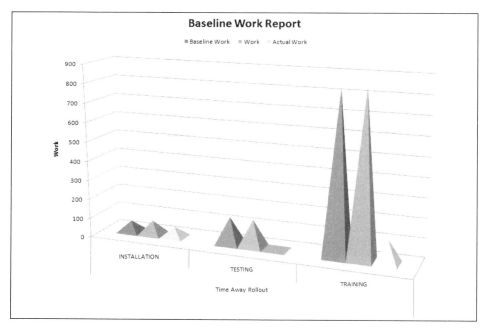

**Figure 4-18: Customized
Baseline Work Report**

6. Save the Baseline Work Report as an Excel Workbook in your student folder and name it *Custom Baseline Work Report.xls*.

7. Close the Baseline Work Report, leave Microsoft Office Excel 2007 open, and then return to your Microsoft Office Project 2007 window.

Saving Local OLAP Cube Data for a Visual Report

After you view the Visual Report and return to Microsoft Office Project 2007, you can save the OLAP cube data by clicking the *Save Data* button at the bottom of the Visual Reports – Create Report dialog. The system displays the Visual Reports – Save Reporting Data dialog shown in Figure 4-19.

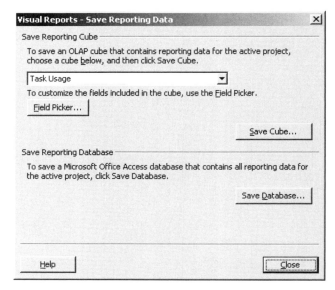

**Figure 4-19: Visual Reports – Save
Reporting Data dialog**

Click the pick list at the top of the dialog and select the local OLAP cube you wish to save. The pick list includes the following OLAP cubes:

- Task Usage
- Resource Usage
- Assignment Usage
- Task Summary
- Resource Summary
- Assignment Summary

Click the *Field Picker* button to select the fields you want included when you save the local OLAP cube. Microsoft Office Project 2007 displays the Visual Reports – Field Picker dialog shown in Figure 4-20. In this dialog, select the standard and custom fields you want included in the OLAP cube and then click the *OK* button.

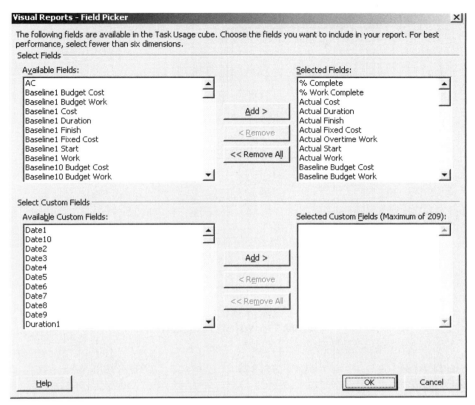

**Figure 4-20: Visual Reports – Field
Picker dialog**

Click the *Save Cube* button when you are ready to save the local OLAP cube. The system saves a file with the .cub file extension. You also have the option to save all of the local OLAP cube information in a Microsoft Office Access 2007 database file by clicking the *Save Database* button. Click the *Close* button when you complete the operation.

Creating Visual Report Templates

Microsoft Office Project 2007 allows you to create your own custom Visual Report templates or to edit any of the default Visual Report templates. The process is very similar whether creating or editing a Visual Report template. To create a new Visual Report template, click the *New Template* button in the Visual Reports – Create Report dialog. The software displays the Visual Reports – New Template dialog shown in Figure 4-21.

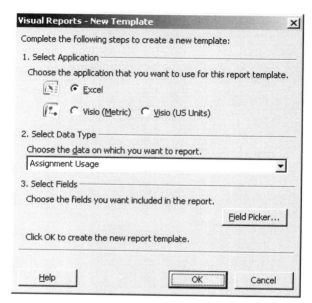

**Figure 4-21: Visual Reports –
New Template dialog**

In the Select Application section, select the *Excel*, the *Visio (Metric)*, or the *Visio (US Units)* option. In the Select Data Type section, click the pick list and select the type of data for your new Visual Report template. In the Select Fields section, click the *Field Picker* button to select the fields to include in the report template. The software displays the Visual Reports – Field Picker dialog, shown previously in Figure 4-20.

 In the Visual Reports – Field Picker dialog, the *Available Fields* list contains several fields denoted as dimension fields. Dimensions are project fields containing values at which the system totals fact data such as Work and Availability. For example, the *Type* field represents the three types of resources available in Microsoft Office Project 2007: Work, Material and Cost.

 Warning: Be judicious when selecting dimensions for your new Visual Report template. Including more than five dimension fields may seriously decrease the performance of your Visual Report.

In the Visual Reports – Field Picker dialog, remove any fields you do not want from the *Selected Fields* list and add additional fields from the *Available Fields* list. You can also add custom fields in your project from the Available Custom Fields section.

 Microsoft Office Project 2007 populates the Visual Reports – Field Picker dialog with the fields appropriate for the data you select for reporting. Most of the time, you can leave the Selected Fields list "as is" and may only need to supplement the fields with custom fields chosen from the Available Custom Fields list.

In the Visual Reports – New Template dialog, click the *OK* button. The system launches Excel 2007 and creates a new workbook with three worksheet tabs. The *Sheet1* tab contains an empty PivotTable and the Field List sidepane contains the fields you selected in the Visual Reports – Field Picker dialog as shown in Figure 4-22.

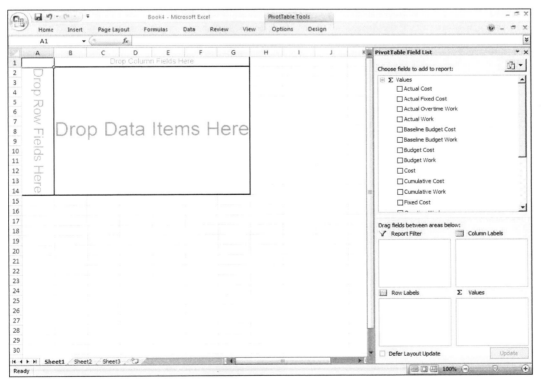

**Figure 4-22: Sheet1 page
with empty PivotTable**

Right-click the *Sheet1* tab and select *Rename* from the shortcut menu to rename the worksheet consistent with the type of Visual Report you want to create. Because I want to create a Work Flow Report similar to the Cash Flow report, I renamed the tab *Task Usage*. Right-click the *Sheet2* tab and delete the worksheet, repeating this action for the *Sheet3* tab as well.

Populate the PivotTable by dragging and dropping fields to the appropriate drop areas at the bottom of the PivotTable Field List sidepane including Report Filter, Column Labels, Row Labels and Values. To populate the Work Flow report PivotTable shown in Figure 4-23, I did the following:

- I dragged the *Tasks* field to the Report Filter drop area.

- I dragged the Time Weekly Calendar to the Row Labels drop area.

- I dragged the *Work* and *Cumulative Work* fields to the Values drop area.

- I dragged the *Σ Values* field from the Row Labels drop area (where it appeared automatically) to the Column Labels drop area.

- I expanded the *Year* field in the PivotTable to show Quarters as well as Years.

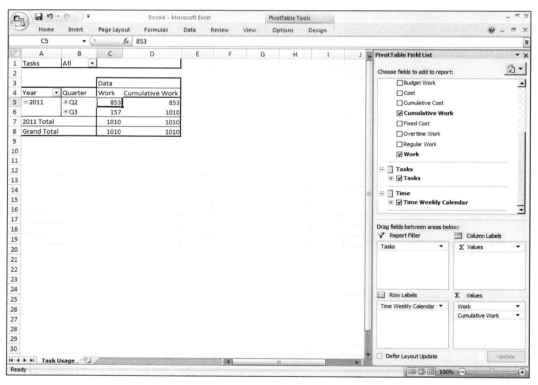

**Figure 4-23: Task Usage page
with populated PivotTable**

Right-click the worksheet tab at the bottom of the page, and then click *Insert* on the shortcut menu. Microsoft Office Excel 2007 displays the Insert dialog shown in Figure 4-24.

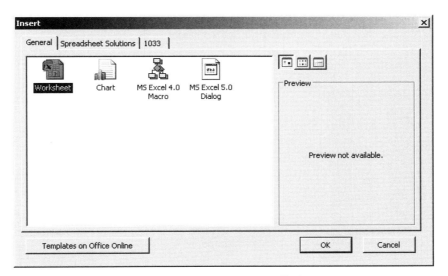

Figure 4-24: Insert dialog

Select the *Chart* icon and then click the *OK* button to insert a generic column chart based on the fields in the PivotTable. Figure 4-25 shows the generic PivotChart. Close both the PivotTable Field List sidepane and the PivotChart Filter Pane window.

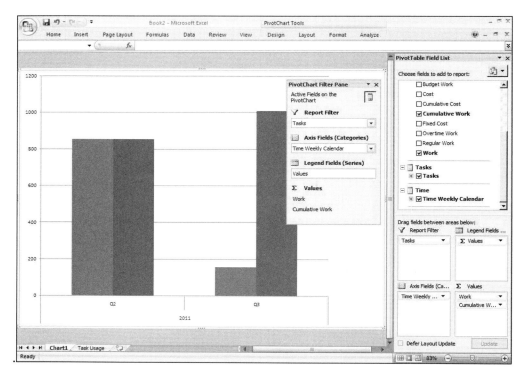

**Figure 4-25: Generic PivotChart
based on PivotTable data**

Click anywhere in the PivotChart to select it and then click the *Layout* menu to display the *Layout* options on the ribbon menu. Using these options, select your settings for one or more of the following:

- Chart Title
- Axis Title
- Legend
- Data Labels
- Axes
- Gridlines

Click the *Design* menu to display the *Design* options on the ribbon menu. Change the *Chart Style* option to meet your requirements. Format any of the PivotChart components to meet your reporting needs. Figure 4-26 shows my completed PivotChart, ready to save as a template.

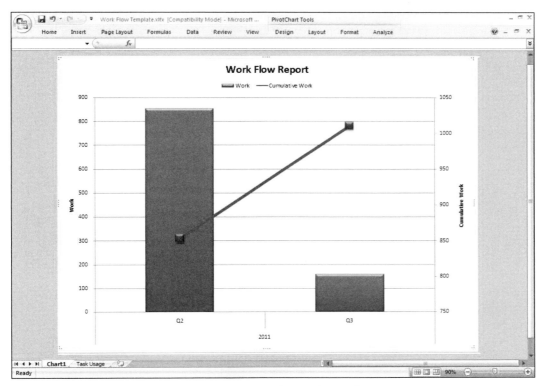

Figure 4-26: PivotChart for
Custom Visual Report Template

When you complete your report design, click the *Save* button. Microsoft Office Excel 2007 displays the Save As dialog and selects the default Template location. In the *File name* field, enter your template name using the name you want to appear in the Visual Reports – Create Template dialog. Click the *Save as type* pick list and select the *Excel template (*.xltx)* option. Click the *Save* button when finished. The software displays the warning dialog about external data in the workbook shown in Figure 4-27. Click the *Yes* button to save the new Visual Report template.

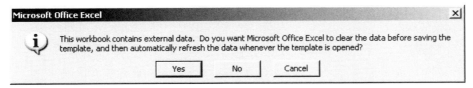

Figure 4-27: External data
warning dialog

When you return to Microsoft Office Project 2007, your new Visual Report template appears on the appropriate tab. Figure 4-28 shows my new Work Flow Report template on the *Task Usage* tab in the Visual Reports – Create Report dialog.

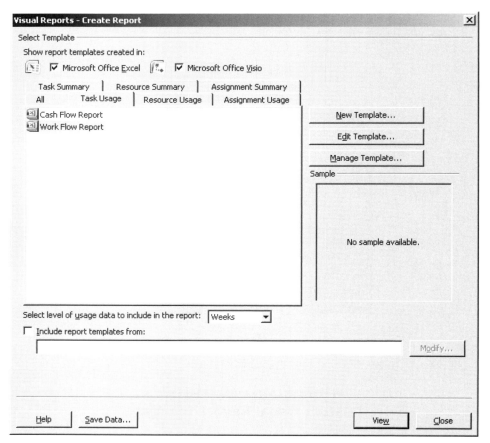

**Figure 4-28: Work Flow Report
on the Task Usage tab**

 All Visual Report templates saved in the default Templates folder automatically appear in the Visual Reports – Create Report dialog. If you save Visual Report templates in any other folder, select the *Include report templates from* option, click the *Modify* button and then navigate to the folder containing the templates.

Editing Visual Report Templates

As I stated earlier, the process of editing a Visual Report template is very similar to the process used to create a Visual Report template. To edit a Visual Report template, select a template and then click the *Edit Template* button in the Visual Reports – Create Report dialog. Microsoft Office Project 2007 displays the Visual Reports – Field Picker dialog. Select the fields you want included in the Visual Report template and then click the *Edit Template* button.

The system launches Microsoft Office Excel 2007 and opens the Visual Report template for editing. Modify the PivotTable and/or PivotChart as you desire, and then click the *Save* button to save the modified Visual Report template.

Hands On Exercise

Exercise 4-4

Create the PivotTable and PivotChart sections of a new Visual Report Template.

1. In the Visual Reports – Create Report dialog, click the *New Template* button.

2. In the Visual Reports – New Template dialog, select the *Excel* option and the *Task Summary* option, and then click the *OK* button.

3. In Microsoft Office Excel 2007, right-click on the *Sheet2* and *Sheet3* worksheet tabs, and then click the *Delete* option on the shortcut menu to remove these extra worksheets.

4. Right-click on the *Sheet1* worksheet tab, click the *Rename* option on the shortcut menu, and name the worksheet as Task Summary.

5. Drag the following fields to the following drop areas in the PivotTable Field List sidepane:

Field Name	Drop Area
Tasks	Report Filter
Actual Work Remaining Work	Values
Σ Values	Row Labels

6. Right-click on the *Task Summary* worksheet tab, click the *Insert* option on the shortcut menu, and then insert a new Chart.

7. Close the PivotTable Field list sidepane and the PivotChart Filter Pane dialog.

Hands On Exercise

Exercise 4-5

Format the PivotChart section of a new Visual Report Template.

1. In Microsoft Office Excel 2007, customize the PivotChart as follows:

   - Click the *Design* menu and then click the *Change Chart Type* button on the ribbon menu.

   - In the Change Chart Type dialog, select the *Exploded pie in 3-D* option (second from the right in the Pie options section) and then click the *OK* button.

   - Right-click the chart Title, select *Edit Text* from the shortcut menu, and rename the Title as *Actual Work vs. Remaining Work*.

   - Click the *Layout* menu, click the *Legend* button on the ribbon menu, and then select the *Show Legend at Top* option.

   - Right-click in either slice of the pie chart and select the *3-D Rotation* option from the shortcut menu.

   - In the Format Chart Area dialog, set the *X Rotation* to *90 degrees*, set the *Y Rotation* to *30 degrees*, and then click the *Close* button.

   - Right-click in either slice of the pie chart and select *Add Data Labels* from the shortcut menu.

   - Right-click either of the Data Labels in the pie chart, and change the font to *14 point* size, *Bold* formatting, with *White* color from the floating *Formatting* menu.

The PivotChart for your Visual Report Template should appear as shown in Figure 4-29.

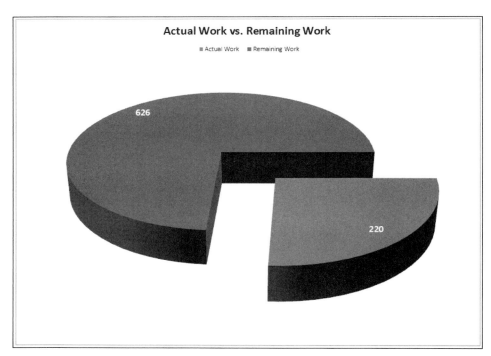

**Figure 4-29: Completed PivotChart for the
new Visual Report Template**

2. Save this workbook as an Excel template (*.xltx) in the default Templates folder and name the template Actual and Remaining Work Report.

3. When the system prompts about external data, click the *Yes* button.

4. Close the Actual and Remaining Work workbook template then close the Excel 2007 application as well.

5. In the Visual Reports – Create Report dialog in Microsoft Office Project 2007, click the Task Summary tab

Your Visual Reports – Create Report dialog should appear as shown in Figure 4-30.

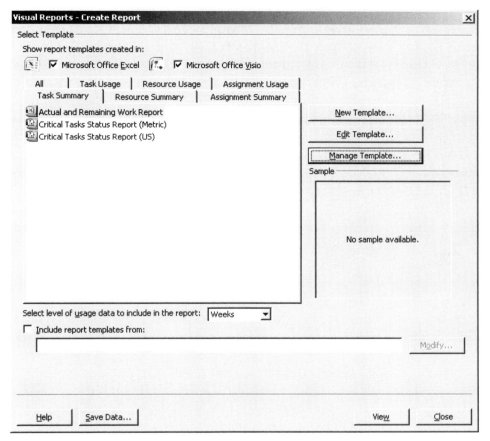

**Figure 4-30: Actual Work and
Remaining Work Report Template**

6. Click the *Close* button to close the Visual Reports – Create Report dialog.

7. Save and close your "Time Away Deployment 04" project file.

Managing Your Visual Report Templates

Click the *Manage Template* button to manage your Visual Report templates. The system opens the default templates folder in a Windows Explorer window as shown in Figure 4-31. From this location, you can rename or delete Visual Report templates as you wish.

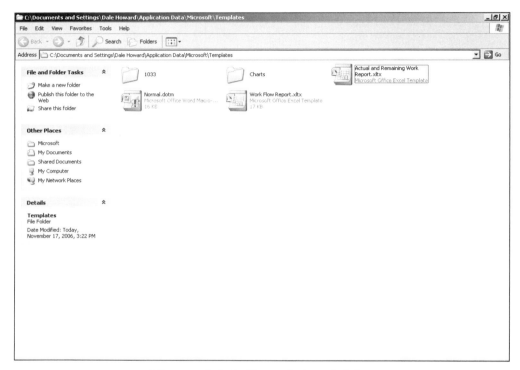

Figure 4-31: Templates folder

Using Cell Background and Text Formatting to Highlight Critical Tasks

Microsoft Office Project 2007 defines the Critical Path as "The series of tasks that must be completed on schedule for a project to finish on schedule." Every task on the Critical Path is a Critical task. By default, all tasks on the Critical Path have a Total Slack of 0 days, which means they cannot slip without delaying the Finish date of the project. If the Finish date of any Critical task slips by even 1 day, the project Finish date slips as well.

Microsoft Office Project 2007 defines a non-Critical task as any task that is 100% complete or any task with a Total Slack greater than 0 days. A non-Critical task can slip by its amount of Total Slack before it delays the Finish date of the project. For example, a task with 5 days of Total Slack can finish 5 days late before the resulting slippage changes the project Finish date.

Microsoft Office Project 2007 automatically calculates the Total Slack for each task to determine the project Critical Path. To view the Total Slack, click View ➤ Table ➤ Schedule to apply the Schedule table. The Total Slack is the last column on the right side of the Table. I discuss the Schedule table later in this module.

In Microsoft Office Project 2007, the Critical Path may run from the Start date to the Finish date of the project, or it may begin anywhere in the project and run to the Finish date of the project. This behavior is a key difference from the traditional Critical Path Method (CPM) of Critical Path definition.

 The Critical Path Method (CPM) defines the Critical Path as the longest-Duration path of tasks through the network of tasks in the project.

 If you make changes to your project by entering actuals or by making plan revisions, your Critical Path may change as well.

Identifying the Critical Path

You can use several methods in Microsoft Office Project 2007 to determine the Critical Path. These methods include:

- Use the Gantt Chart Wizard to display the Critical Path in the Gantt Chart view.
- Apply the Tracking Gantt view.
- Temporarily insert the Critical task field in any task Table.
- Apply text formatting or cell background formatting.
- Use a default or custom Filter.

You can use a default filter, along with Cell Background Formatting or text formatting, to highlight tasks on the critical path. To use text formatting, complete the following steps:

1. Click Format ➤ Text Styles.

Microsoft Office Project 2007 displays the Text Styles dialog shown in Figure 4-32.

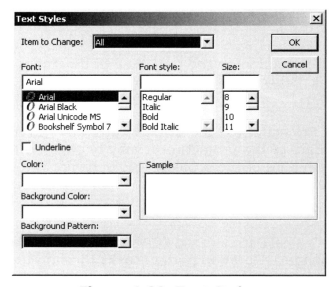

**Figure 4-32: Text Styles
dialog**

2. Click the *Item to Change* pick list and select the *Critical Tasks* item from the list.

3. Set the *Font*, *Font style* and *Size* options as you wish.

4. Click the *Color* pick list and select a different color for Critical task text.

5. Click the *OK* button.

Microsoft Office Project 2007 formats the text for Critical tasks as shown in Figure 4-33.

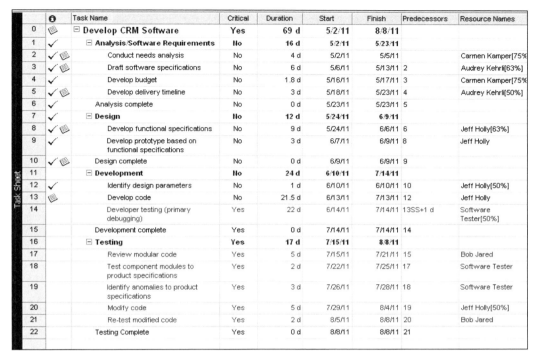

	❶	Task Name	Critical	Duration	Start	Finish	Predecessors	Resource Names
0	🖻	⊟ Develop CRM Software	Yes	69 d	5/2/11	8/8/11		
1	✓	⊟ Analysis/Software Requirements	No	16 d	5/2/11	5/23/11		
2	✓🖻	Conduct needs analysis	No	4 d	5/2/11	5/5/11		Carmen Kamper[75%]
3	✓🖻	Draft software specifications	No	6 d	5/6/11	5/13/11	2	Audrey Kehrli[63%]
4	✓	Develop budget	No	1.8 d	5/16/11	5/17/11	3	Carmen Kamper[75%]
5	✓🖻	Develop delivery timeline	No	3 d	5/18/11	5/23/11	4	Audrey Kehrli[50%]
6	✓	Analysis complete	No	0 d	5/23/11	5/23/11	5	
7	✓	⊟ Design	No	12 d	5/24/11	6/9/11		
8	✓🖻	Develop functional specifications	No	9 d	5/24/11	6/6/11	6	Jeff Holly[63%]
9	✓	Develop prototype based on functional specifications	No	3 d	6/7/11	6/9/11	8	Jeff Holly
10	✓🖻	Design complete	No	0 d	6/9/11	6/9/11	9	
11		⊟ Development	No	24 d	6/10/11	7/14/11		
12	✓	Identify design parameters	No	1 d	6/10/11	6/10/11	10	Jeff Holly[50%]
13	🖻	Develop code	No	21.5 d	6/13/11	7/13/11	12	Jeff Holly
14		Developer testing (primary debugging)	Yes	22 d	6/14/11	7/14/11	13SS+1 d	Software Tester[50%]
15		Development complete	Yes	0 d	7/14/11	7/14/11	14	
16		⊟ Testing	Yes	17 d	7/15/11	8/8/11		
17		Review modular code	Yes	5 d	7/15/11	7/21/11	15	Bob Jared
18		Test component modules to product specifications	Yes	2 d	7/22/11	7/25/11	17	Software Tester
19		Identify anomalies to product specifications	Yes	3 d	7/26/11	7/28/11	18	Software Tester
20		Modify code	Yes	5 d	7/29/11	8/4/11	19	Jeff Holly[50%]
21		Re-test modified code	Yes	2 d	8/5/11	8/8/11	20	Bob Jared
22		Testing Complete	Yes	0 d	8/8/11	8/8/11	21	

**Figure 4-33: Text for Critical tasks
formatted in red in the Task Sheet view**

The other method of displaying the Critical Tasks is to apply the new Project 2007 cell background formatting, by completing the following steps:

1. Click Format ➢ Text Styles.

2. Click the *Item to Change* pick list and select the *Critical Tasks* item from the list.

3. Set the *Font*, *Font style,* and *Size* options as you wish.

4. Set the *Background Color* and the *Background Pattern* options.

5. If necessary, click the *Color* pick list and select a color that contrasts with the Background Color you selected.

6. Click the *OK* button.

Figure 4-34 shows the Text Styles dialog after setting the *Background Color* option to *Red*, the text *Color* option to *White,* and the *Font style* option to *Bold*.

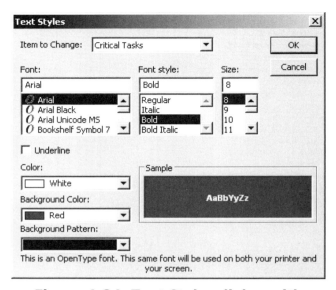

**Figure 4-34: Text Styles dialog with
cell background formatting
options selected**

Figure 4-35 shows the project with text and background cell formatting applied.

	❶	Task Name	Critical	Duration	Start	Finish	Predecessors	Resource Names
0	🖉	⊟ **Develop CRM Software**	Yes	69 d	5/2/11	8/8/11		
1	✓	⊟ **Analysis/Software Requirements**	No	16 d	5/2/11	5/23/11		
2	✓🖉	Conduct needs analysis	No	4 d	5/2/11	5/5/11		Carmen Kamper[75%
3	✓🖉	Draft software specifications	No	6 d	5/6/11	5/13/11	2	Audrey Kehrli[63%]
4	✓	Develop budget	No	1.8 d	5/16/11	5/17/11	3	Carmen Kamper[75%
5	✓🖉	Develop delivery timeline	No	3 d	5/18/11	5/23/11	4	Audrey Kehrli[50%]
6	✓	Analysis complete	No	0 d	5/23/11	5/23/11	5	
7	✓	⊟ **Design**	No	12 d	5/24/11	6/9/11		
8	✓🖉	Develop functional specifications	No	9 d	5/24/11	6/6/11	6	Jeff Holly[63%]
9	✓	Develop prototype based on functional specifications	No	3 d	6/7/11	6/9/11	8	Jeff Holly
10	✓🖉	Design complete	No	0 d	6/9/11	6/9/11	9	
11		⊟ **Development**	No	24 d	6/10/11	7/14/11		
12	✓	Identify design parameters	No	1 d	6/10/11	6/10/11	10	Jeff Holly[50%]
13	🖉	Develop code	No	21.5 d	6/13/11	7/13/11	12	Jeff Holly
14		**Developer testing (primary debugging)**	**Yes**	**22 d**	**6/14/11**	**7/14/11**	**13SS+1 d**	**Software Tester[50%]**
15		Development complete	Yes	0 d	7/14/11	7/14/11	14	
16		⊟ **Testing**	Yes	17 d	7/15/11	8/8/11		
17		**Review modular code**	**Yes**	**5 d**	**7/15/11**	**7/21/11**	**15**	**Bob Jared**
18		**Test component modules to product specifications**	**Yes**	**2 d**	**7/22/11**	**7/25/11**	**17**	**Software Tester**
19		**Identify anomalies to product specifications**	**Yes**	**3 d**	**7/26/11**	**7/28/11**	**18**	**Software Tester**
20		**Modify code**	**Yes**	**5 d**	**7/29/11**	**8/4/11**	**19**	**Jeff Holly[50%]**
21		**Re-test modified code**	**Yes**	**2 d**	**8/5/11**	**8/8/11**	**20**	**Bob Jared**
22		Testing Complete	Yes	0 d	8/8/11	8/8/11	21	

**Figure 4-35: Cell background formatting
applied to Task Sheet view for Critical tasks**

Text and cell background formatting are attributes of the View in which you apply them. When you apply formatting to a task, Microsoft Office Project 2007 applies formatting to the task for all Tables you apply **in the current View only**.

For example, if you apply the Aqua cell background color to a task displayed in the Gantt Chart view, the software applies the background formatting to the task in every task Table you apply in the Gantt Chart view such as the Cost and Work tables. However, if you display the Tracking Gantt view, the system does not apply the formatting to the task. This means that you can apply different formatting to a task by applying it in a different View.

Hands On Exercise

Exercise 4-6

Use text formatting and background cell formatting to determine the Critical Path.

1. Return to your "Analyze Critical Path" project file.

2. Click View ➤ More Views and then apply the Task Sheet view.

3. Click Format ➤ Text Styles.

4. For the *Critical Tasks* item, set the following values and then click the *OK* button:

Font Style	Bold
Color	White
Background Color	Red
Background Pattern	Solid (black)

Your project should appear as shown in Figure 4-36.

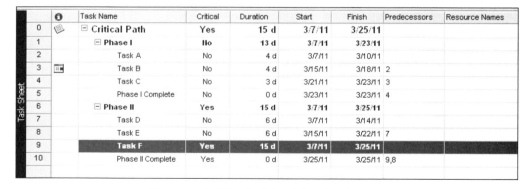

	🛈	Task Name	Critical	Duration	Start	Finish	Predecessors	Resource Names
0	📝	⊟ Critical Path	Yes	15 d	3/7/11	3/25/11		
1		⊟ Phase I	No	13 d	3/7/11	3/23/11		
2		Task A	No	4 d	3/7/11	3/10/11		
3	🔲	Task B	No	4 d	3/15/11	3/18/11	2	
4		Task C	No	3 d	3/21/11	3/23/11	3	
5		Phase I Complete	No	0 d	3/23/11	3/23/11	4	
6		⊟ Phase II	Yes	15 d	3/7/11	3/25/11		
7		Task D	No	6 d	3/7/11	3/14/11		
8		Task E	No	6 d	3/15/11	3/22/11	7	
9		**Task F**	**Yes**	**15 d**	**3/7/11**	**3/25/11**		
10		Phase II Complete	Yes	0 d	3/25/11	3/25/11	9,8	

**Figure 4-36: Critical task shown
with cell background formatting**

5. Change the Task F Duration to 10 days.

Notice in Figure 4-37 that the cell background formatting changes because Task B and Task C are now Critical tasks.

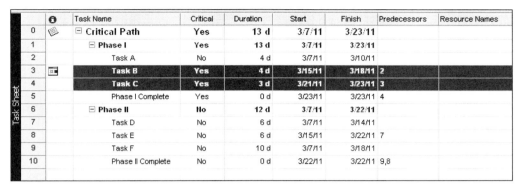

		❶	Task Name	Critical	Duration	Start	Finish	Predecessors	Resource Names
	0	🖉	⊟ Critical Path	Yes	13 d	3/7/11	3/23/11		
	1		⊟ Phase I	Yes	13 d	3/7/11	3/23/11		
	2		Task A	No	4 d	3/7/11	3/10/11		
	3	▣◼	**Task B**	**Yes**	**4 d**	**3/15/11**	**3/18/11**	**2**	
	4		**Task C**	**Yes**	**3 d**	**3/21/11**	**3/23/11**	**3**	
	5		Phase I Complete	Yes	0 d	3/23/11	3/23/11	4	
	6		⊟ Phase II	No	12 d	3/7/11	3/22/11		
	7		Task D	No	6 d	3/7/11	3/14/11		
	8		Task E	No	6 d	3/15/11	3/22/11	7	
	9		Task F	No	10 d	3/7/11	3/18/11		
	10		Phase II Complete	No	0 d	3/22/11	3/22/11	9,8	

**Figure 4-37: New Critical tasks shown
with cell background formatting**

6. Save and close your "Analyze Critical Path" project file.

Module 05

What's New Miscellaneous

Learning Objectives

After completing this module, you will be able to:

- Understand changes in how the cost field is displayed in the Assign Resources dialog

- Understand how to save Microsoft Office Project 2007 files in earlier versions of the software

- Understand which file formats are now available for exporting project data

- Understand changes in field names in EVA task tables

Using the Cost Field in the Assign Resources Dialog

The Cost column is a new feature in Microsoft Office Project 2007 that provides two capabilities not included in previous versions of the software:

1. When you select a resource using the Assign Resource dialog and click the *Assign* button, the software shows you the cost for that task assignment for that resource, based on the resource standard rate.

2. When you assign a Cost resource to a task or to a summary task, you can enter the estimated cost for that Cost resource in this column. The software allows you to assign a cost when assigning an Expense Cost resource.

To access the Assign Resources dialog, use either of the following methods:

• Click the *Assign Resources* button ⬛ on the *Standard* toolbar.

• Click Tools ➤ Assign Resources.

Figure 5-1 shows the initial view of the Assign Resources dialog. Notice the *Cost* column at the right edge of the data grid.

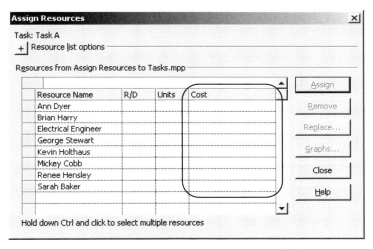

**Figure 5-1: Assign Resources dialog
Resource list options hidden**

Saving Project Files in Earlier Versions

Microsoft Office Project 2007 uses a **different** file format than that used in Microsoft Project 2000, 2002, and 2003. The Microsoft Office Project 2007 file format is **not** backward compatible with prior versions of the software. If you want your Microsoft Office Project 2007 file accessible to users of Microsoft Project 2000-2003, then you must save your project in a compatible format using the following steps when you save the file:

1. Click File ➤ Save.

2. In the Save As dialog, click the *Save as type* pick list and select the *Project 2000 – 2003 (*.mpp)* option, as shown in Figure 5-2.

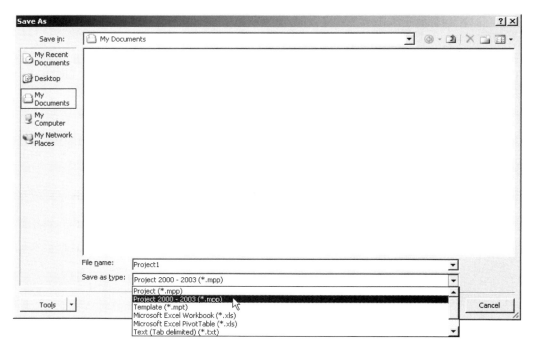

**Figure 5-2: Save As dialog, save a
file using the Project 2000-2003 format**

1. Type a name for your project that conforms to your company's naming convention.

2. Click the *Save* button.

The software displays the warning dialog shown in Figure 5-3.

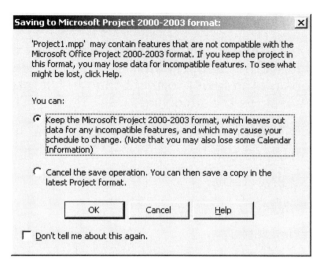

**Figure 5-3: Warning dialog shown
when saving to Project 2000-2003 format**

3. In the warning dialog, select the first option and then click the *OK*
button.

 Saving the file using the Microsoft Project 2000-2003
format omits features found only in Microsoft Office
Project 2007.

Exporting Project Data

Microsoft Office Project 2007 allows you to export project data to a variety of file formats readable by other applications. Microsoft Office Project 2007 permits you to export data in fewer formats than in Microsoft Project 2000-2003. These formats include the following:

- Microsoft Project 2000-2003
- Microsoft Excel Workbook
- Microsoft Excel PivotTable
- Text (Tab delimited)
- CSV (Comma delimited)
- XML Format

 The Microsoft Project 2000-2003 file format provides "backwards compatibility" with earlier versions of the software.

 Previous versions of the software allowed you to save a project file as a Web page (*.html or *.htm), Project Database (*.mpd), Access database (*.mdb), or to literally any ODBC compliant database. Microsoft Office Project 2007 no longer supports saving project files to database file formats. Instead, Microsoft expects you to use the XML format for exchanging data with database applications.

To save a project file in another file format, complete the following steps:

1. Click File ➤ Save As.

Microsoft Office Project 2007 displays the Save As dialog shown in Figure 5-4.

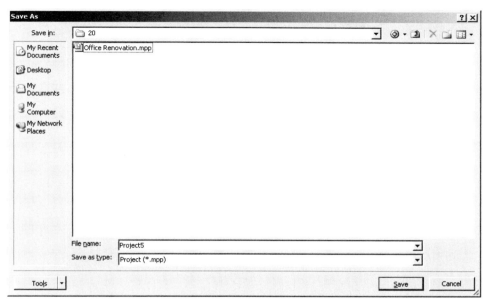

Figure 5-4: Save As dialog

2. In the Save As dialog navigate to the folder to save the file.

3. In the Save As dialog click the *Save as type* pick list and select the file type such as the *Microsoft Excel Workbook (*.xls)* shown in Figure 5-5.

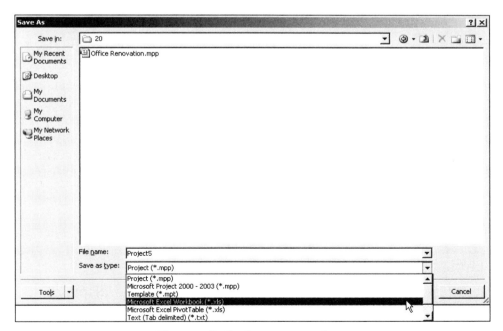

**Figure 5-5: Save a project
as a Microsoft Excel Workbook**

4. Click the *Save* button.

Microsoft Office Project 2007 displays the Export Wizard Welcome page shown in Figure 5-6.

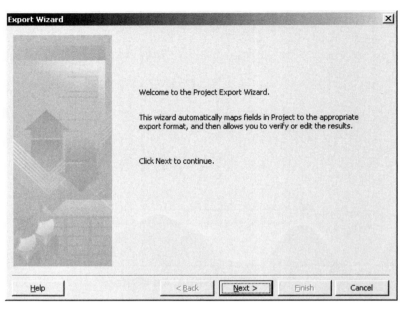

**Figure 5-6: Export Wizard
Welcome page**

From this point on, the Export Wizard is the same as it was in Microsoft Project 2000-2003.

Understanding the New Earned Value Fields

According to Microsoft Office Project 2007 Help, Earned Value is a "measure of the cost of work performed up to the status date or current date. Earned value uses your original cost estimates saved with a baseline and your actual work to date to show whether the actual costs incurred are on budget." You use Earned Value Analysis (EVA) to measure project performance and to analyze project variance. Microsoft Office Project 2007 provides you with a number of calculated EVA fields.

While Microsoft has not changed the task sequence for setting up Microsoft Office Project 2007 for EVA from prior versions of the software, Microsoft has made some changes in the names of fields in the three task Tables that display Earned Value Analysis information.

Microsoft Office Project 2007 offers three task Tables that display Earned Value Analysis information. These Tables are:

- Earned Value
- Earned Value Cost Indicators
- Earned Value Schedule Indicators

Before you apply any of the EVA tables, you should apply the Task Sheet view because each EVA table contains many columns. To apply the Task Sheet view, click View ➢ More Views. In the More Views dialog, select the Task Sheet view and then click the *Apply* button.

To apply the Earned Value table, click View ➢ Table ➢ More Tables. In the More Tables dialog, select the Earned Value table and then click the *Apply* button. Figure 5-7 shows the Earned Value table. Microsoft changed the names of the first three column titles only; all other titles are unchanged.

	Task Name	Planned Value - PV (BCWS)	Earned Value - EV (BCWP)	AC (ACWP)	SV	CV	EAC	BAC	VAC
0	⊟ Develop CRM Software	$15,000.00	$9,207.13	$8,550.00	($5,792.88)	$657.13	$23,215.72	$25,000.00	$1,784.28
1	⊟ Analysis/Software Requirements	$3,600.00	$3,600.00	$3,300.00	$0.00	$300.00	$3,300.00	$3,600.00	$300.00
2	Conduct needs analysis	$1,500.00	$1,500.00	$1,200.00	$0.00	$300.00	$1,200.00	$1,500.00	$300.00
3	Draft software specifications	$1,200.00	$1,200.00	$1,200.00	$0.00	$0.00	$1,200.00	$1,200.00	$0.00
4	Develop budget	$500.00	$500.00	$500.00	$0.00	$0.00	$500.00	$500.00	$0.00
5	Develop delivery timeline	$400.00	$400.00	$400.00	$0.00	$0.00	$400.00	$400.00	$0.00
6	Analysis complete	$0.00	$0.00	$0.00	$0.00	$0.00	$0.00	$0.00	$0.00
7	⊟ Design	$3,600.00	$3,600.00	$3,650.00	$0.00	($50.00)	$3,650.00	$3,600.00	($50.00)
8	Develop functional specifications	$2,000.00	$2,000.00	$1,850.00	$0.00	$150.00	$1,850.00	$2,000.00	$150.00
9	Develop prototype based on functional specifications	$1,600.00	$1,600.00	$1,800.00	$0.00	($200.00)	$1,800.00	$1,600.00	($200.00)
10	Design complete	$0.00	$0.00	$0.00	$0.00	$0.00	$0.00	$0.00	$0.00
11	⊟ Development	$7,800.00	$2,007.13	$1,600.00	($5,792.88)	$407.13	$9,565.92	$12,000.00	$2,434.08
12	Identify design parameters	$200.00	$200.00	$200.00	$0.00	$0.00	$200.00	$200.00	$0.00
13	Develop code	$5,200.00	$1,116.25	$600.00	($4,083.75)	$516.25	$4,300.11	$8,000.00	$3,699.89
14	Developer testing (primary debugging)	$2,400.00	$690.88	$800.00	($1,709.13)	($109.13)	$4,400.22	$3,800.00	($600.22)
15	Development complete	$0.00	$0.00	$0.00	$0.00	$0.00	$0.00	$0.00	$0.00
16	⊟ Testing	$0.00	$0.00	$0.00	$0.00	$0.00	$5,800.00	$5,800.00	$0.00
17	Review modular code	$0.00	$0.00	$0.00	$0.00	$0.00	$2,000.00	$2,000.00	$0.00
18	Test component modules to product specifications	$0.00	$0.00	$0.00	$0.00	$0.00	$800.00	$800.00	$0.00
19	Identify anomalies to product specifications	$0.00	$0.00	$0.00	$0.00	$0.00	$1,200.00	$1,200.00	$0.00
20	Modify code	$0.00	$0.00	$0.00	$0.00	$0.00	$1,000.00	$1,000.00	$0.00
21	Re-test modified code	$0.00	$0.00	$0.00	$0.00	$0.00	$800.00	$800.00	$0.00
22	Testing Complete	$0.00	$0.00	$0.00	$0.00	$0.00	$0.00	$0.00	$0.00

**Figure 5-7: Earned Value table
in the Task Sheet view**

Microsoft Office Project 2007 displays the following three fields with new names in the task Earned Value table:

- **BCWS** - The new name for the BCWS (Budgeted Cost of Work Scheduled) field is **Planned Value – PV (BCWS)**. This field contains the cumulative timephased baseline costs up to the Status Date.

- **BCWP** - The new name for the BCWP (Budgeted Cost of Work Performed) field is the **Earned Value – EV (BCWP)**. This field contains the cumulative value of the percent complete multiplied by the timephased baseline costs calculated up to the Status Date.

- **ACWP** - The new name of the ACWP (Actual Cost of Work Performed) field is **AC (ACWP)**. This field shows the total actual costs incurred on the task up to the Status Date.

Figure 5-8 shows the Earned Value Cost Indicators table. In that table, Microsoft has changed the names of the first two column titles only; all other titles remain unchanged.

		Task Name	Planned Value - PV (BCWS)	Earned Value - EV (BCWP)	CV	CV%	CPI	BAC	EAC	VAC	TCPI
	0	⊟ **Develop CRM Software**	**$15,000.00**	**$9,207.13**	**$657.13**	**7%**	**1.08**	**$25,000.00**	**$23,215.72**	**$1,784.28**	**0.96**
	1	⊟ **Analysis/Software Requirements**	**$3,600.00**	**$3,600.00**	**$300.00**	**8%**	**1.09**	**$3,600.00**	**$3,300.00**	**$300.00**	**0**
	2	Conduct needs analysis	$1,500.00	$1,500.00	$300.00	20%	1.25	$1,500.00	$1,200.00	$300.00	0
	3	Draft software specifications	$1,200.00	$1,200.00	$0.00	0%	1	$1,200.00	$1,200.00	$0.00	1
	4	Develop budget	$500.00	$500.00	$0.00	0%	1	$500.00	$500.00	$0.00	1
	5	Develop delivery timeline	$400.00	$400.00	$0.00	0%	1	$400.00	$400.00	$0.00	1
	6	Analysis complete	$0.00	$0.00	$0.00	0%	0	$0.00	$0.00	$0.00	0
	7	⊟ **Design**	**$3,600.00**	**$3,600.00**	**($50.00)**	**-1%**	**0.99**	**$3,600.00**	**$3,650.00**	**($50.00)**	**-0**
	8	Develop functional specifications	$2,000.00	$2,000.00	$150.00	7%	1.08	$2,000.00	$1,850.00	$150.00	0
	9	Develop prototype based on functional specifications	$1,600.00	$1,600.00	($200.00)	-13%	0.89	$1,600.00	$1,800.00	($200.00)	-0
	10	Design complete	$0.00	$0.00	$0.00	0%	0	$0.00	$0.00	$0.00	0
	11	⊟ **Development**	**$7,800.00**	**$2,007.13**	**$407.13**	**20%**	**1.25**	**$12,000.00**	**$9,565.92**	**$2,434.08**	**0.96**
	12	Identify design parameters	$200.00	$200.00	$0.00	0%	1	$200.00	$200.00	$0.00	1
	13	Develop code	$5,200.00	$1,116.25	$516.25	46%	1.86	$8,000.00	$4,300.11	$3,699.89	0.93
	14	Developer testing (primary debugging)	$2,400.00	$690.88	($109.13)	-16%	0.86	$3,800.00	$4,400.22	($600.22)	1.04
	15	Development complete	$0.00	$0.00	$0.00	0%	0	$0.00	$0.00	$0.00	0
	16	⊟ **Testing**	**$0.00**	**$0.00**	**$0.00**	**0%**	**0**	**$5,800.00**	**$5,800.00**	**$0.00**	**1**
	17	Review modular code	$0.00	$0.00	$0.00	0%	0	$2,000.00	$2,000.00	$0.00	1
	18	Test component modules to product specifications	$0.00	$0.00	$0.00	0%	0	$800.00	$800.00	$0.00	1
	19	Identify anomalies to product specifications	$0.00	$0.00	$0.00	0%	0	$1,200.00	$1,200.00	$0.00	1
	20	Modify code	$0.00	$0.00	$0.00	0%	0	$1,000.00	$1,000.00	$0.00	1
	21	Re-test modified code	$0.00	$0.00	$0.00	0%	0	$800.00	$800.00	$0.00	1
	22	Testing Complete	$0.00	$0.00	$0.00	0%	0	$0.00	$0.00	$0.00	0

**Figure 5-8: Earned Value Cost Indicators
table in the Task Sheet view**

Microsoft Office Project 2007 displays the following two fields with new names in the task Earned Value Cost Indicators table:

- **BCWS** - The new name for the BCWS (Budgeted Cost of Work Scheduled) field is **Planned Value – PV (BCWS)**. This field contains the cumulative timephased baseline costs up to the Status Date.

- **BCWP** - The new name for the BCWP (Budgeted Cost of Work Performed) field is the **Earned Value – EV (BCWP)**. This field contains the cumulative value of the percent complete multiplied by the timephased baseline costs calculated up to the Status Date.

Figure 5-9 shows the Earned Value Schedule Indicators table where Microsoft changed the names of the first two column titles only; all other titles are unchanged.

		Task Name	Planned Value - PV (BCWS)	Earned Value - EV (BCWP)	SV	SV%	SPI
	0	⊟ **Develop CRM Software**	**$15,000.00**	**$9,207.13**	**($5,792.88)**	**-39%**	**0.61**
	1	⊟ **Analysis/Software Requirements**	**$3,600.00**	**$3,600.00**	**$0.00**	**0%**	**1**
	2	Conduct needs analysis	$1,500.00	$1,500.00	$0.00	0%	1
	3	Draft software specifications	$1,200.00	$1,200.00	$0.00	0%	1
	4	Develop budget	$500.00	$500.00	$0.00	0%	1
	5	Develop delivery timeline	$400.00	$400.00	$0.00	0%	1
	6	Analysis complete	$0.00	$0.00	$0.00	0%	0
	7	⊟ **Design**	**$3,600.00**	**$3,600.00**	**$0.00**	**0%**	**1**
	8	Develop functional specifications	$2,000.00	$2,000.00	$0.00	0%	1
	9	Develop prototype based on functional specifications	$1,600.00	$1,600.00	$0.00	0%	1
Task Sheet	10	Design complete	$0.00	$0.00	$0.00	0%	0
	11	⊟ **Development**	**$7,800.00**	**$2,007.13**	**($5,792.88)**	**-74%**	**0.26**
	12	Identify design parameters	$200.00	$200.00	$0.00	0%	1
	13	Develop code	$5,200.00	$1,116.25	($4,083.75)	-79%	0.21
	14	Developer testing (primary debugging)	$2,400.00	$690.88	($1,709.13)	-71%	0.29
	15	Development complete	$0.00	$0.00	$0.00	0%	0
	16	⊟ **Testing**	**$0.00**	**$0.00**	**$0.00**	**0%**	**0**
	17	Review modular code	$0.00	$0.00	$0.00	0%	0
	18	Test component modules to product specifications	$0.00	$0.00	$0.00	0%	0
	19	Identify anomalies to product specifications	$0.00	$0.00	$0.00	0%	0
	20	Modify code	$0.00	$0.00	$0.00	0%	0
	21	Re-test modified code	$0.00	$0.00	$0.00	0%	0
	22	Testing Complete	$0.00	$0.00	$0.00	0%	0

**Figure 5-9: Earned Value Schedule Indicators
table in the Task Sheet view**

Microsoft Office Project 2007 displays the following two fields with new names in the task Earned Value Schedule Indicators table:

- **BCWS** - The new name for the BCWS (Budgeted Cost of Work Scheduled) field is **Planned Value – PV (BCWS)**. This field contains the cumulative timephased baseline costs up to the Status Date.

- **BCWP** - The new name for the BCWP (Budgeted Cost of Work Performed) field is the **Earned Value – EV (BCWP)**. This field contains the cumulative value of the percent complete multiplied by the timephased baseline costs, calculated up to the Status Date.

Hands On Exercise

Exercise 5-1

Study the Earned Value Analysis (EVA) fields in a project.

1. Open the "Earned Value Analysis" project file from your student folder.

2. Click Project ➤ Project Information and set the *Status Date* field to 10/7/11 representing the last day of the previous reporting period.

3. Click View ➤ More Views and apply the Task Sheet view.

4. Click View ➤ Table ➤ More Tables and apply the Earned Value table.

5. Float your mouse pointer over each indicator (to the left of the Task Name column) to determine the current status of each task and then study the Earned Value fields to see how they reflect the status of each task.

6. Click View ➤ Table ➤ More Tables and apply the Earned Value Cost Indicators table and study the current status of each task.

7. Click View ➤ Table ➤ More Tables and apply the Earned Value Schedule Indicators table and study the current status of each task.

8. Save and close your "Earned Value Analysis" project file.

Module 06

What's New Macros

Learning Objectives

After completing this module, you will be able to:

- Add an undo transaction to a macro
- Undo a macro containing a transaction set in Microsoft Office Project 2007

Undoing Macros

Microsoft Office Project VBA (Visual Basic for Applications) is a mini-programming language built into Microsoft Office Project 2007 and other Microsoft applications. Project VBA provides full support for many new features in Microsoft Office Project 2007. A macro is a script (program) that automates multiple-step activities within Microsoft Office Project 2007 that would otherwise be difficult or impossible to execute manually. Many a project manager has run a macro without first saving a copy of their file and then regretted it upon seeing the results. The new support for multi-level undo for macros eliminates that horror. Microsoft Office Project 2007 has multiple levels of undo, as described in Module 03. The number of undo levels defaults to 20, but the following statement, when used in a macro increases the levels to 30:

```
Application.UndoLevels = 30
```

Every time VBA code executes an undoable action, the system adds a new undo record to the undo list. If your macro performs 50 undoable actions, then with 30 undo levels set the system loses the ability to undo the first 20 undo actions. Despite increasing the undo levels above 50, you must then interpret a very long undo list to determine where your macro begins and ends.

Thankfully, Project 2007 VBA allows you to group undoable actions together by creating a named transaction set under one name such as FormattingMacro, for example. This causes the system to display the entire group as one name in the Undo list. You can then undo all the macro's actions in one easy undo. If you are writing macros intended for use by others, this provides a much cleaner way for the user to work with your macro.

To group many actions together, you need to create an Undo Transaction Set. To create an Undo Transaction Set copy and edit the code in Code 6-1.

```
Sub CreateUndoTransaction()
    Application.OpenUndoTransaction "Macro Changes"

    'Insert code that changes your project here

    Application.CloseUndoTransaction
End Sub
```

Code 6-1: Transaction set skeleton code

125

The following code sample shown in Code 6-2 is an edited version that simply adds 3 Tasks to a project.

```
Sub CreateUndoTransaction()
    Application.OpenUndoTransaction "Macro Changes"

    ActiveProject.Tasks.Add "Macro Inserted Task 1"
    ActiveProject.Tasks.Add "Macro Inserted Task 2"
    ActiveProject.Tasks.Add "Macro Inserted Task 3"

    Application.CloseUndoTransaction
End Sub
```

Code 6-2: Transaction Set adds three tasks to the project

Figure 6-1 shows a project where a User entered Task 1 then ran a macro to add Tasks 2-4. The macro creates a transaction called **Macro Changes** to capture all Task additions. When you click the *Undo* pick list button, you see Macro Changes at the top, as the most recent action. Click the *Macro Changes* item and the system removes all Tasks inserted by the macro.

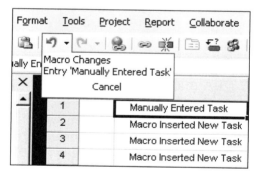

Figure 6-1: Undo list with the Macro Changes transaction

 Undoing a macro undoes the result of the entire macro and not just each of the macro steps individually.

 msProjectExperts recommends that you capture the changes your macro makes to a project file in a VBA Undo Transaction, which allows the user to undo the results all at once.

Hands On Exercise

Exercise 6-1

Use new features in Project 2007 VBA code. **Note:** For this exercise, you need Microsoft Office Project 2007 Standard or Professional.

1. Open the Macro Sample.mpp file from your student folder.

2. Select Tools ➤ Macro ➤ Macros.

3. Select the CreateUndoTransaction macro in the Macro dialog and then click the *Run* button.

> If the *Run* button is grayed out in the Macro dialog after you select the CreateUndoTransaction macro, you may have to change your macro security by taking the following steps:
>
> 1. Click Tools ➤ Macro ➤ Security.
> 2. In the Security dialog, select the *Low* option.
> 3. Click the *OK* button.
> 4. Exit and Restart Project 2007.

4. Notice that the macro adds three new tasks to the blank project.

5. Click the *Undo* button.

6. Notice that the software removes the added tasks.

7. Close the Macro Sample.mpp file.

Index

CONSULTING

TRAINING

BOOKS AND COURSEWARE

SUPPORT

You deserve the best, don't settle for less! MSProjectExperts is a Microsoft Certified Partner specializing in Microsoft Office Project Server since its first release. This is not something we "also do," it's all we do. Our consultants are recognized by Microsoft as being among the world's top experts with three Microsoft Project MVPs on staff.

MSProjectExperts

90 John Street, Suite 404

New York, NY 10038

(646) 736-1688

To learn more about MSProjectExperts:

http://www.msprojectexperts.com

For the best Project and Project Server training available:

http://www.projectservertraining.com

To learn more about our books:

http://www.projectserverbooks.com

For FAQs and other free support:

http://www.projectserverexperts.com

You may also need these books!

Buy direct from our website or your favorite bookseller

Managing Enterprise Projects using Microsoft Office Project Server 2007, ISBN 978-1-934240-02-1

Implementing and Administering Microsoft Office Project Server 2007, ISBN 978-1-934240-01-4

Ultimate Learning Guide to Microsoft Office Project 2007,
ISBN 978-1-934240-00-7

VBA Programming for Microsoft Office Project versions 98 through 2007, ISBN 0-9759828-7-7

Administering Microsoft Office Project Server 2003,
ISBN 978-1-934240-03-8

Managing Enterprise Projects using Microsoft Office Project Server 2003, Second Edition, ISBN 978-0-9759828-9-1

ᴍsProjectExperts provides a complete line of Microsoft Office Project and Project Server courseware covering every role in the enterprise. Each book has its own Instructor documentation and file downloads to support classroom training or self-study. Contact us at (646) 736-1688 for more information or visit our website at
http://www.msprojectexperts.com